BLACK HISTORY MATTERS

Robin Walker

W

FRANKLIN WATTS
LONDON•SYDNEY

Editor: Julia Bird
Designer: Emma DeBanks
Consultant: Dr Onyeke Nubia, writer, lecturer and historian

ISBN 978 1 4451 6690 2

Picture credits:
AF Archive/Alamy: front cover cbl. AKG Images/Pictures from History: 7. Vladimir B Aleks/Shutterstock: 8t. Sven Steffen Amdt/CC Wikimedia Commons: 11t. Apatow Productions/Columbia Pictures/Superstock: 25t. Barcroft Media/Getty Images:39t. Cristiano Barni/Shutterstock front cover tl. A Bell, 1773. PD Wikimedia Commons: 36-37b. Yann Arthus-Betrand/Getty Images: 19t. Bikeworldtravel/Shutterstock: 64t. James Boardman Archive/Alamy: front cover bc, 4. Bournemouth News/Rex Features/Shutterstock: 17b. Trustees of the British Museum, London: 28. Kristin Cato/Alamy: 58b. B.N.Chagny/Sociétéde Géographie de Genève: 10b. Chronicle/Alamy: 34tr. Dmitry Chulov/Dreamstime: 17tl. Civitates orbis terrarum, 1572/PD Wikimedia Commons: 26b, 65bl. Classical Numismatic Group/CC Wikimedia Commons: 17tr. CloudyStock/Shutterstock: front cover br. Contraband Collection/Alamy: 54-55c. Matt Crossick/Alamy 61b. db Images/Alamy: front cover cl. Detroit Institute of Art/Bridgeman Images: 39br. Diego G Diaz/Shutterstock 58t. Discott/CC Wikimedia Commons: 24c. DOD Photo/Alamy: 59. DPPI Media/Alamy 60b. Dreamworks Film Company/AF Archive/Alamy: 34bl. Everett Collection/Alamy: front cover tl & cbr. Everett Historical/Shutterstock: 29t, 30-31t. 35, 36bl, 43t, 49t, 50, 53t. Ewa Studio/Shutterstock: 14-15b. Five Hundred Thousand Strokes for Freedom, 1853/PD Wikimedia Commons: 32b. Gado Images/Alamy: front cover bcl. GL Archive/Alamy: 42r. Glasshouse Images/Rex Features/Shutterstock: 48. Granger Historical PA/Alamy: front cover bl, & c, 21cr, 38c. Granger/Rex Features/Shutterstock: 30bl, 51t, 51b, 52b, 59. Grove Press: 45bc. Neil Harrison/Dreamstime: 15cr. Homo Cosmicus/Shutterstock: 29b. Peter Horree/Alamy: 13t, 22-23. Kathy Hutchins/Shutterstock: 53b. Interfoto/Alamy: 10cr. ITV/Rex Features/Shutterstock: 54bl. iulias/Shutterstock: front and back cover bg. javaman/Shutterstock: 8-9b. Markus Keffler/Rex Features/Shutterstock: 47t. Keystone/Alamy: 44-45c. Keystone/Hulton/Getty Images: 46b. trevor kittlelty/Shutterstock: front cover cblc. Asmus Koefoed/Shutterstock: 30br. John Warburton-Lee/Alamy: 27tr. The Life Collection/Getty Images: 45t. LOC/Abdul Kader Haidera: 19b. Martchan/Shutterstock: 58b. Niday Picture Library/Alamy: 41b. North Wind Picture Archives/Alamy: 37b. Gianni Dagli Orti/Rex Features/Shutterstock: 14bl. Christine Osborne Pictures/Alamy: 27tl. PA Archive/PA Images: 57b. PA Images/Alamy: 61t. PAC45: 43b. PAL/Topfoto: 45br, 65br. Rahel Patrasso/Xinhua/Alamy: 33b. Photogenes: 23cr. Picturegroup/Rex Features/Shutterstock: 58t. Tom Pilston/The Independent/Rex Features/Shutterstock: 58t. Rex Features/Shutterstock: 31b. Ryuk/Shutterstock: 9cr. Science History Images/Alamy: 48-49c. Sipa/Rex Features /Shutterstock: 56b. Sodatech/Superstock: 11b. Joseph Sohm/Shutterstock: front cover cr, 5. Superstock: 16. Ben Thornley/Shutterstock 60t. Trinity Mirror/Mirrorpix/Alamy: 20bg, 55t, 65t. Universal History Archive/UIG/Rex Features/Shutterstock: 40b. Richard Wareham Fotografie/Alamy: 33l. PD Wikimedia Commons: Catalan Atlas, sheet 6, 1375, 18; 25b, 42b. WitR/Shutterstock: 13b. World History Archive/Alamy: 9bc, 12. Yaroslaff/Shutterstock: 46t. Michael Zagaris/Getty Images: front cover clc. Ariadne Van Zandbergen/Alamy: 20b.

The website addresses (URLs) included in this book were valid at the time of going to press. However, it is possible that contents or addresses may have changed since the publication of this book. No responsibility for any such changes can be accepted by either the author or the Publisher.

Franklin Watts
An imprint of
Hachette Children's Group
Part of Hodder & Stoughton
Carmelite House
50 Victoria Embankment
London EC4Y 0DZ

An Hachette UK Company
www.hachettechildrens.co.uk

MIX
Paper from
responsible sources
FSC® C104740
www.fsc.org

CONTENTS

WHY BLACK HISTORY MATTERS

Black history is a vital part of world history. Understanding the struggles and battles of the past helps us to understand and make sense of the world today. Yet for far too long, Black history has been neglected, its lessons and experiences ignored and overlooked.

THE MURDER OF STEPHEN LAWRENCE

On 22 April 1993, Stephen Lawrence, a Black British teenager from south London, was murdered in an unprovoked racist attack. The killing took place in Eltham, south-east London as Stephen and his friend Duwayne Brooks waited for a bus. Five white men were widely believed to have carried out the attack and were arrested by the police, but they were not charged.

Judge Sir William Macpherson led a public enquiry into the handling of the case in 1998. He found that the Metropolitan Police were institutionally racist. Eventually, two of the suspects were brought to trial in 2011 and convicted in 2012.

WHAT IS BLACK HISTORY?

Black history is the record of how people of African descent have shaped the world around them. It includes the cities, nation states, empires and political entities that African people created. It includes the art, literature and cultural heritage they left behind. It is also the record of African resistance to being conquered, dominated and discriminated against.

A photo of Stephen Lawrence issued by the police.

4

People take part in a Black Lives Matter street protest in Los Angeles, USA, in 2015.

THE DEATH OF TRAYVON MARTIN

On 26 February 2012, Trayvon Martin, an unarmed African-American teenager, was shot dead in Sanford, Florida, USA. As Martin walked to the home of a family friend, George Zimmerman, a member of the local neighbourhood watch, spotted him and called the police, saying that Martin looked suspicious. Zimmerman claimed he then got into a fight with Martin. During the fight Zimmerman shot Martin in the chest, killing him. The Florida police initially refused to charge Zimmerman. But when media all over the world began reporting on the story, the Florida authorities were embarrassed into investigating. Zimmerman was eventually found not guilty of murder or manslaughter on 13 July 2013.

BLACK LIVES MATTER

Members of the African-American community responded to the acquittal of George Zimmerman by beginning a new protest movement: Black Lives Matter, designed to raise awareness of and end ongoing injustice towards Black people. Founded by three African-American women, the movement organises online campaigns, street demonstrations and protests. It also draws attention to other controversial killings of African-Americans at the hands of the police and other authorities. Black Lives Matter has now become a global force.

FLASHPOINTS

The deaths of Stephen Lawrence and Trayvon Martin proved defining moments in race relations. Their deaths raise many questions that are looked at in this book. What did the people responsible for their deaths think of people of African descent? If society had a better sense of Black history, would it help to improve how we interact today?

5

THE LANDS OF THE PHARAOHS

The story of Black history begins in North Africa, in the fertile lands surrounding the River Nile.

TA-SETI

The Nubian kingdom of Ta-Seti is believed to be the oldest African kingdom yet discovered. Archaeologists working at Qustul, near the modern Egyptian and Sudanese border, discovered evidence of Ta-Seti in 1962 when they found tombs belonging to a dynasty of pharaohs (kings and queens) of Nubia who may have ruled around 3400 BCE. In 1979, a researcher published the evidence of Ta-Seti in the *New York Times*. Nubia, not Egypt as so often believed, was now seen as the starting point for African history.

MEDITERRANEAN SEA

LIBYAN DESERT

Giza • • Heliopolis
Saqqara •
Memphis •

Hermopolis •

EGYPT

Abydos •
Western Thebes • • Karnak
• Edfu

• Aswan

TA-SETI

Qustul •

River Nile

Kerma •

RED SEA

White Nile

Blue Nile

Adule •

This map shows the Nubian kingdom of Ta-Seti and Old Kingdom Egypt.

Dates in this book

Some historians accept a different dating system, where the Old Kingdom period spanned 5660–4188 BCE, rather than 3100–2181, pushing the dates further back in time. So that readers can use this book alongside other resources, it uses the more commonly accepted dating system.

Period	Dates used in this book	Alternative dates
Kingdom of Ta-Seti Dynasty	c.3400 BCE	c.5900 BCE
Old Kingdom Period (Dynasties 1 to 6)	3100 to 2181 BCE	5660 to 4188 BCE
Kerma Period in Kush	c.2500 to 1500 BCE	c.4200 to 1661 BCE
Middle Kingdom Period (Dynasties 11 to 12)	2040 to 1786 BCE	3448 to 3182 BCE
Second Intermediate Period: (Dynasties 13 to 17)	1786 to 1560 BCE	3182 to 1709 BCE
New Kingdom Period (Dynasties 18 to 20)	1560 to 1080 BCE	1709 to 1095 BCE
Late Kushite Period	860 BCE to 350 CE	860 BCE to 350 CE

DISCOVERING TA-SETI

The tombs at Qustul contained around 5,000 artefacts, which helped archaeologists to learn more about how the Ta-Setians lived. The Ta-Setians made most of the artefacts themselves. They acquired others by trading with their neighbours around the Red Sea, central Sudan, Egypt and the Middle East. Boats are depicted in their art and this shows how people travelled around. Five different styles of pottery were also found. These helped the archaeologists to date the site by comparing the pottery to ancient Egyptian pottery. They found that the first of the nine or 11 Ta-Setian pharaohs ruled 200 or 300 years before the first pharaoh of Egypt. Some ceramics also featured fragments of hieroglyphic script, some of the oldest writing in the world.

TREASURES OF THE TOMBS

Gold pieces found in the tombs included a bracelet and a necklace with a fly-shaped pendant, proving that the Ta-Setians wore fine jewellery. Copper artefacts included a mace and spearheads, used to wage war, as well as a tray and a cap for a furniture leg. The ivory pieces included spoons and gaming pieces. Also found was a wooden gaming board, probably used to play a game called senet, which was a little like backgammon. Other artefacts included terracotta and limestone hippos, one hundred stone vessels and four thousand objects made from seashells.

FAMOUS ARCHERS

Ta-Seti means 'Land of the bow', indicating that the Ta-Setians used bows and arrows to hunt and to wage war.

ANCIENT EGYPT

The most famous of the ancient African kingdoms centred around Egypt (also known as Kemet) and began around 5,000 years ago.

MONUMENTAL MONUMENTS

The oldest Egyptian stone monument is now an archaeological site found at Saqqara in northern Egypt. Known as Gisr el Mudir, or the Enclosure of the Boss, it is believed to have been built around 2770 BCE. No one knows exactly what it was used for, but its size is staggering at 650 by 350 metres. Dating from around 2670 BCE is the Funerary Complex of Saqqara. Fragments of its 1.5 km perimeter wall still exist. Inside are columns and courts. The centrepiece is the Step Pyramid, standing 60 metres tall and built of six huge steps.

Later, in the Fourth Dynasty Period, the ancient Egyptians built the Step Pyramid of Meidum, the Bent and Red Pyramids of Dahshur, and, most famously, the three Pyramids of Giza, near the modern city of Cairo. The Great Pyramid of Giza is as tall as a 40-storey building. Another celebrated monument is the Sphinx of Giza (far right). Carved in the shape of a lion, it has an African head wearing a pharaonic headdress. Archaeologists are divided about how old it is. Many believe it is around 4,500 years old; others contend it may be more than 7,000 years old.

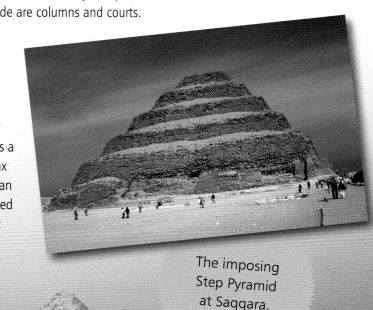

The imposing Step Pyramid at Saqqara.

The pyramids of Giza were built to display the wealth of Egypt's pharaohs.

BUILDERS AND CRAFTERS

What does all this building tell us about the ancient Egyptians? Clearly, their masons excelled in mathematics, engineering and architecture. They believed it was important to build religious tombs and monuments that would last. Egypt was wealthy and could afford to use its resources and employ workers to build such lavish buildings, many of which can still be visited today.

The ancient Egyptians were also skilled at making crafts. They created portrait sculptures, ranging in size from tiny figurines to giant colossi such as the Sphinx of Giza, and decorated their temples with paintings of people, from royals to ordinary people. Like the Ta-Setians, they created superb gold jewellery. They also carved inscriptions and other writings.

WRITERS AND THINKERS

The ancient Egyptian writings and inscriptions help to build a picture of life in their time. The *Edwin Smith Papyrus*, named after the dealer who bought it, is a copy of a text from around 3000 BCE that describes 48 cases of head and neck surgery. Pharaoh Unas, who ruled from 2345 TO 2315 BCE, commissioned a pyramid with walls carved with inscriptions. Known as the *Pyramid Texts*, it contains the spells and hymns the pharaoh will need in his afterlife. It also claims that earth, air, fire and water are the building blocks of creation, ideas that later influenced the ancient Greeks (see p.14). The *Prisse Papyrus* contains a copy of a book called the *Maxims of Ptahhotep*. In it, Ptahhotep, a top adviser to the pharaoh, explains how individuals should behave with wisdom and humility when dealing with all people.

The columns at Saqqara are the first known columns to have been built.

The Great Sphinx at Giza is believed to have the face of the Pharaoh Khafre (c.2558–2532 BCE).

HIEROGLYPHS

Hieroglyphs were one ancient Egyptian form of writing. Hieroglyphs were signs that represented objects, symbols for objects or symbols for sounds. Altogether there were believed to be over 1,000 different hieroglyphs.

KUSH

The kingdom of Kush absorbed the previous Nubian kingdom of Ta-Seti (see p.6–7) and became the dominant African state south of Egypt from around 2500–1500 BCE. It was a political rival to Old and Middle Kingdom Egypt.

CAPITAL KERMA

Kush was located close to both the River Nile and Red Sea, bringing trading opportunities, and it had gold and emerald mines, giving it wealth and influence. Archaeologists continue to excavate Kush's capital, Kerma. They have discovered the city walls, their rectangular towers and fortified gates. Protected inside were the gardens, the palace of the king, the houses of the nobility and a big religious complex that also housed bronze workshops.

Kush's decline was linked to the disappearance of its water supply. The two Nile channels that used to feed Kerma dried up and the city suffered. A final blow came with the rise of Egypt's 18th dynasty of pharaohs whose military campaigns destroyed Kerma.

A Kushite glass vessel with gold script, dating from the 3rd century CE.

An aerial view of Kerma, the ancient capital city of Kush.

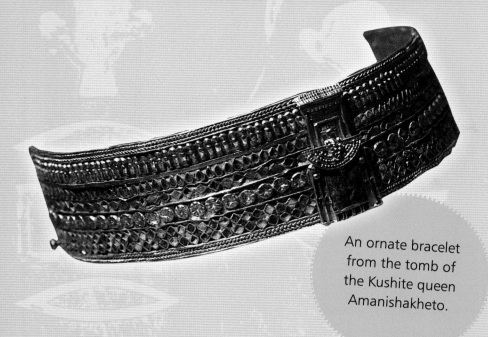

An ornate bracelet from the tomb of the Kushite queen Amanishakheto.

RETURN TO GREATNESS

Kush flourished a second time between 860 BCE and CE 350. During this time, the Kushites built at least 220 pyramids in the cities of Al Kurru, Nuri, Gebel Barkal and Meroë. Following their conquest of Egypt in around 716 BCE, they placed their female relatives on the thrones of Egypt. Shepenoupet II was one such ruler, and the last independent Black ruler of Egypt. Her name appears on the monuments and temples restored during her time. Before this period, however, five women had ruled Egypt as pharaohs.

A NEW CAPITAL

The capital of Kush was moved further south to the city of Meroë, on the banks of the River Nile, from 590 BCE until CE 350, following an invasion from Egypt. Meroë was famous as a centre of trade in Kush, excelling in metalworks, and rich in resources such as wood and grain. Remains discovered there include 84 pyramids and the ruins of a bath house. In the 4th century CE, however, Meroë was captured by the Axumites (now part of Ethiopia) and Kush declined once more.

WRITING AND NUMBERS

From the 4th century BCE, the Kushites invented a new script called Meroïtic. There are 900 surviving documents in this script. Some are stone inscriptions. Others were written on papyri. Unfortunately, scholars are unable to interpret these writings as Meroïtic has not yet been deciphered. The Kushites also invented a numerical system for mathematics.

This stele shows Queen Amanishakheto (right) with the goddess Amesemi.

11

EGYPT THRIVES
AND DECLINES

Ancient Egypt flourished once more during the Middle Kingdom period, from 2040 to 1786 BCE. Upper and Lower Egypt were reunited during this time under Mentuhotep II, the founder of the Middle Kingdom.

ARTS AND ARCHITECTURE

The Middle Kingdom was seen as a golden age of Egyptian culture, where art, literature and science thrived. During this era, the Egyptians wrote the *Rhind Mathematical Papyrus* which contains 87 mathematical problems and their solutions. Waset became the capital city, where 11 pharaohs from the 11th and 12th dynasties ruled. They built the Labyrinth at Hawwara in Middle Egypt with its 3,000 apartments and 12 palaces. Another great achievement was the construction of the city of Kahun with its horizontal and vertical road plan and five 70-room mansions. Unfortunately, these are archaeological sites now, with only ruins remaining.

THE PHARAOHS LOSE CONTROL

Following the collapse of the Middle Kingdom soon after the death of female Pharaoh Sobekneferu in around 1786 BCE, Egypt went into a period of decline. The pharaohs lost power over the regions, called nomes, to such an extent that they became independent of royal authority. This allowed invaders from the Middle East an opportunity to take over. Historians call this the Second Intermediate Period. During this time a total of 217 pharaohs ruled over 226 years of chaos. Half of these rulers were from the Middle East.

Mentuhotep II (right) ruled Egypt for around 50 years and is remembered for bringing the country together.

A NEW WORLD

The ancient Egyptian New Kingdom lasted from around 1560 to 1080 BCE and was ruled by 31 pharaohs, including some of the most famous rulers, such as Ramesses II and Queen Hatshepsut. Egypt was now at the height of its political power. Its rulers conquered many lands in the Middle East and Kush to the south. Wealth flowed into the country from Kush, as well as the more distant lands of Syria and Crete.

GROWING POPULATION

Though Egypt now contained Middle Eastern populations who had arrived in the Second Intermediate Period (see p.12), studies show that the ruling families of this period were Africans. As during the Middle Kingdom, they continued to build. Waset, the capital city, grew to house a population of one million people, while the wealth of the pharaohs at this time paid for huge temples at Karnak and Luxor. Outside Waset, Pharaoh Ramesses II commissioned the Abu Simbel Temple (below), painstakingly carved out of a mountain.

Queen Ahmose-Nefertiti (right) ruled Egypt alongside her husband, Pharaoh Ahmose I. They started the New Kingdom Period.

The temple of Abu Simbel is found on the bank of the River Nile. It is now a UNESCO World Heritage Site.

EBERS PAPYRUS

An important New Kingdom era text has survived. The *Ebers Papyrus* is believed to be the oldest medical encyclopaedia in the world. It covers eye, skin and intestinal diseases, as well as obstetrics and dentistry.

13

NORTH AFRICAN
INVASIONS

From the end of the rule of Shepenoupet II (see p.11) who was deposed by Assyrians from the Middle East in 663 BCE, until it declared independence in 1922, Egypt was under foreign control. After being ruled by the Assyrians, Egypt was occupied by the Persians, the Greeks, the Romans, and finally, the Arabians. Each ruling country left its own legacy on the Egyptian civilisation.

PERSIAN RULE

The Persians came from modern-day Iran. They ruled Egypt from 525 BCE. During their time in power, they allowed Greek scholars to live and study in Egypt. Among the Greeks who arrived were the historian Herodotus, the philosophers Democritus and Plato, and the philosopher and mathematician Pythagoras. From their visits, the Greeks learned and developed the theory from the *Pyramid Texts* (see p.9) that earth, air, fire and water were the building blocks of creation.

JEWEL OF THE NILE

The Nile region, with its rich soils, was very fertile and was an ideal place to grow grain crops. Consequently, Egypt developed a reputation as the breadbasket of the ancient world. When foreign invaders entered Egypt, the good quality soils encouraged many to stay.

The Greek historian Herodotus (c.484–425 BCE) wrote extensively about Egypt.

ANCIENT GREEKS AND ROMANS

The Greeks claimed Egypt from the Persians in 332 BCE and became its next ruling class. During this time, the city of Alexandria (named for Alexander the Great) was founded and flourished, boasting the famous Lighthouse of Alexandria. Significant agricultural reforms were also made. Three hundred years later, the mighty Romans took control of Egypt from the last Greek ruler, Cleopatra VII, in 30 BCE, and went on to conquer the whole of North Africa. Ruling for 600 years, they dominated and even enslaved the original people of North Africa. Egypt was one of their most prized provinces, bringing the Roman Empire lots of wealth, while Alexandria was the empire's second biggest city after Rome. Egyptians were themselves able to become Roman citizens. Some of them rose to high positions in the Roman administration, the army and the Christian Church.

ARABIAN INVASION

Following the long decline of the vast Roman Empire, the Arabians entered North Africa in CE 639 as the new conquerors. They recorded that two populations lived there, the white overlords they called 'Greeks', and indigenous populations who resembled each other: Egyptian, Ethiopian, Nubian or African Jews. Like the Romans before them, the Arabs dominated and enslaved the indigenous people of North Africa. These conquests and enslavement whitened North Africa as the indigenous peoples fled further south.

The Arabian invaders introduced Islam into Africa. This religion went on to profoundly influence African culture. Islam was spread across North Africa by conquerors, and was brought to West Africa and East Africa by traders and merchants.

The land around the Nile is especially fertile as the annual floods bring rich river silt onto the floodplain.

The last pharaoh Cleopatra VII (left) with Caesarion, her son with the Roman leader Julius Caesar.

15

ETHIOPIA

Another African kingdom with a long and rich history is Ethiopia. Historians believe that there was trade between Egypt and Ethiopia as long ago as 3,500 BCE. Unlike Egypt, Ethiopia has been independent for most of its existence.

TRADE AND POWER

Ethiopia grew rich from trading goods such as ivory, rhinoceros horn, gold and silver across the Nile and Red Sea regions. From around the 7th century BCE, the kingdom of D'mt grew up, but little is known about it, and it was superceded in around the 1st century CE by the powerful kingdom of Axum.

GREAT BUILDINGS

Ethiopia is very rich in architectural heritage. The Temple of Almaqah in Yeha, D'mt's capital, is the oldest monument in the country and was built before 500 BCE. Axum, the next capital, has seven giant obelisks that date between the 3rd century BCE and the 3rd century CE.

PREHISTORIC FIND

The skeletal remains of one of the oldest ancestors of humanity was found in Ethiopia in 1974. It belonged to a female who lived over three million years ago. Palaeontologists have named her Lucy.

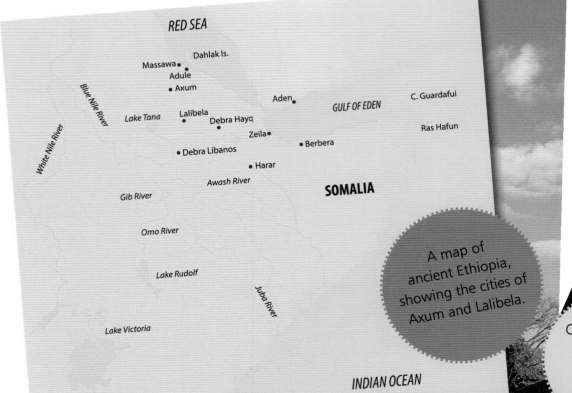

A map of ancient Ethiopia, showing the cities of Axum and Lalibela.

One of the famous Axum obelisks. It stands over 23 metres tall.

MONEY MAKERS

The Axumites minted coins of gold, silver or bronze from the 3rd century CE. Few nations at the time minted their own coins. The coins name 20 early rulers of Ethiopia. In CE 330 Christianity was introduced to Ethiopia by the Saint Frumentius, who later became the first Bishop of Axum. The Axumite King Ezana converted to Christianity and issued coins featuring the Christian cross that said "May the country be satisfied!"

These gold coins show the Axumite king Eon. They were minted in around CE 400.

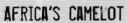

COLOSSAL CHURCHES

In the 12th and 13th centuries CE, Lalibela, in the heart of Ethiopia, became the new capital of the country. Lalibela contains 11 churches carved out of the mountain rock by hammer and chisel. The largest is the House of the Redeemer, which is surrounded by a forest of columns, all carved and sculpted. Lalibela is not the only place to have such wonders. There are 3,000 such churches dotted across Ethiopia and neighbouring Eritrea.

The church of St George in Lalibela. The 11 churches are a site of pilgrimage for Christians.

The index to the *Abba Garima Gospels*. These precious books are kept in a monastery in Ethiopia.

AFRICA'S CAMELOT

In the 17th century the northern city of Gondar became the new Ethiopian capital. It had schools, churches, gardens, pools and zoos and became known as 'the Camelot of Africa', because of its 11 castles, which were built from the 17th century onwards. However, the British invaded Ethiopia in 1868 and took many precious artefacts from these ancient sites. Some Gondar artefacts are now in London museums and include precious manuscripts, church art, gold and silver treasures and intricate royal crowns.

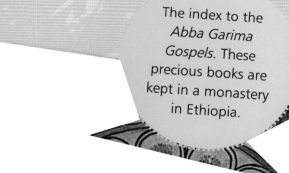

THE WRITTEN WORD

Ethiopia has 250,000 surviving ancient manuscripts. One of them, the *Abba Garima Gospels,* is the oldest illustrated Christian manuscript in the world, written between CE 330 and 650. Ethiopia also has calendar manuscripts, dating from the 4th to the 19th centuries. Its monks kept complex calendars to measure time in blocks of 532 years. Other manuscripts show a knowledge of astronomy, recording solar eclipses in 1241, 1528 and 1727, and a lunar eclipse in 1620.

THE WEST AFRICAN DESERT EMPIRES

Ancient Ghana was the first major empire in West Africa. Beginning in around CE 300 with the first of its 44 kings, Ghana became an African superpower in the 10th and 11th centuries, ruling half of West Africa. The great West African empires of Mali and Songhai developed later.

Mansa Musa I of Mali is believed to have been the richest ruler who ever lived, with an estimated fortune of around £310 billion.

GHANA

Ancient Ghana grew through trade. It was well placed to control the camel and donkey trading caravans and two rivers – the Niger and Senegal – that brought gold, salt, leather products and books into and through its realms.

The capital of ancient Ghana, Kumbi Saleh, was described as a twin city divided by religion. In the royal township, the people followed the traditional religion, involving the honouring of their ancestors. In the other township, the people followed the 'new' religion of Islam.

MALI

Mali was the successor to ancient Ghana in West Africa. Beginning as a kingdom under Ghanaian rule in CE 800, Mali became a power in its own right by 1240. By the 14th century, it was one of the largest empires in the world. Founded by the military brilliance of Sundiata Keita, and then Mansa Musa I, two generations later, the Malian armies conquered half of West Africa. Mali's wealth centred around trade, particularly in the gold that came from its three huge mines, but also in salt and copper. Islam was the official religion of government, but traditional ancestral religions were also practised.

SONGHAI

Following Mali's decline, Songhai seized much of its territory to take over as the next major empire in West Africa. Like Ghana and Mali before it, the Songhai Empire controlled important trade routes. Songhai's great wealth was to prove its downfall. In around 1591 a Moroccan army invaded, intent on seizing Songhai's gold and the great empire fell.

SLAVES

Slavery was an important part of Songhai's empire-building. Many slaves were prisoners of war. However, if they converted to Islam after capture, they could not be sold as slaves.

BUILDINGS AND HERITAGE

The cities of Djenné, Timbuktu and Gao, located in today's Mali, have preserved some of Mali and Songhai's heritage. Archaeologists have found that in Gao from the 10th to the 14th century they had the technology to make glass windows. Djenné has thousands of two-storey hand-sculpted houses from the 15th and 16th centuries with drainage pipes and toilets. By contrast, there were other great cities at the time, such as London, where inhabitants still emptied human waste out of their windows! In the centre of Djenné stands the Grand Mosque. First constructed in the 11th century as a palace, it became a mosque in 1204. The largest clay brick building in the world, there are copies of it all over the world.

LEARNING

Timbuktu and Djenné both had famous universities. Timbuktu's university was centred at the Sankoré Mosque and may have dated from the 11th century. Scholars came from all over the world to study there. The Sankoré Mosque famously appears as the fictional capital of Wakanda in the 2018 blockbuster film *Black Panther*.

Libraries from the universities of Timbuktu and Djenné are still managed by African families and institutions. There are 700,000 medieval manuscripts in Timbuktu alone. Most are in Arabic which was then the international language of scholarship. The manuscripts cover topics as varied as Islamic law, astronomy and poetry.

A librarian in Timbuktu displays a huge collection of medieval manuscripts.

AHMED BABA: FAMOUS SCHOLAR

Professor Ahmed Baba is often described as one of the greatest African scholars. He was born in Timbuktu in 1556. As a child, he memorised the Koran. Later he studied the classic texts of Islam, grammar and calculus.

In 1591, Sultan Ahmad Al Mansur from Morocco ordered the invasion of Timbuktu. In October 1593, Mansur ordered the arrest of the Timbuktu scholars. Baba and his family were captured and sent to Morocco in chains. Baba complained bitterly that his precious library of 1,600 books were seized by the army.

Eventually, the Moroccans released Baba on the condition that he must remain in Marrakech. There he wrote 29 papers, taught at the university and became the country's top judge. His rulings were regarded as final. In 1607, Baba was allowed to return home. He continued teaching in Timbuktu until his death in 1627. He is remembered and celebrated today for his wisdom and fairness, as well as his bravery in standing up to the Moroccan invaders.

A painting believed to be of Ahmed Baba.

THE NIGERIA REGION

In ancient times, Nigeria did not exist as a country. The region of West Africa it is found in, however, has a very rich heritage.

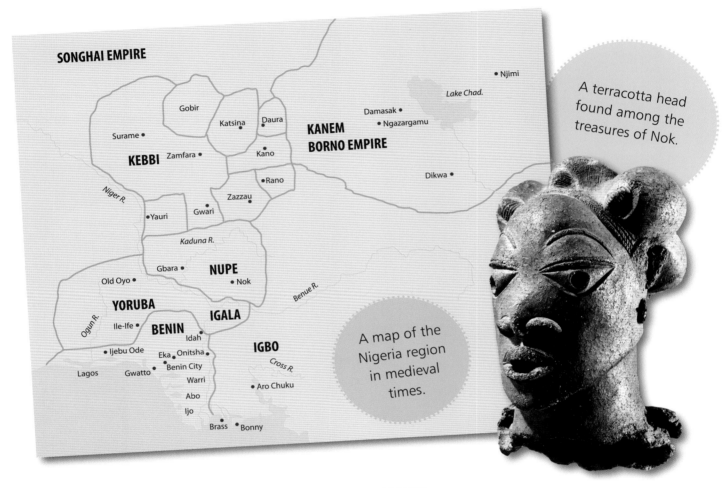

A map of the Nigeria region in medieval times.

A terracotta head found among the treasures of Nok.

NOK

Tin miners, in what is now the Benue Plateau of Nigeria, first discovered evidence of an ancient Iron Age civilisation in 1928 when they stumbled upon some terracotta sculptures and figurines of people and animals. Historians now call this long-lost civilisation 'Nok' and date the art pieces from 1000 to 300 BCE. Other artefacts were later found, including iron and stone tools and weapons.

YORUBA

The Yoruba kingdoms existed from 600 to about CE 1500 in the form of city-states. The Yoruba introduced growing yams, making cheese and breeding horses to West Africa. They had brilliant metal-workers, weavers, carvers and potters. The Yoruba capital city was called Ile-Ife. According to Yoruba mythology, the queen Olowu had the city's roads paved in around CE 1000 after her robes were muddied while walking in the city's streets.

BENIN

While the mighty empire of Songhai was growing across the desert region, the kingdom of Benin was developing along the West African coast. Led by a succession of five warrior kings known as obas, Benin grew in power and influence throughout the 15th and 16th centuries. Unusually, it traded not only with its African neighbours, but also with Europe, in goods such as cotton, palm oil and animal skins, as well as slaves. In return, Benin was able to buy manufactured guns from Europe, with which it could defend itself. Benin's capital, Benin City, also boasted an enormous defensive wall and moat.

DESTRUCTION

By the 1860s, Benin's power had declined. It was also at risk from the British who wanted to take over the region for its rich resources, including rubber, palm oil and ivory. In 1897, the British invaded Benin and made it part of the British Empire. They burned the capital to the ground, destroying much of the empire's heritage. During British rule, any rebuilding of the Benin palace complex was banned. Only in Hausaland, northern Nigeria, were medieval monuments left intact, including the city of Kano, the royal palace complexes of Daura, Kano and Katsina and the Great Mosque of Zaria in Zazzau.

This bronze plaque shows an oba of Benin with his attendants. It dates from the 16th century.

CRAFTS

Benin's craft workers were organised into groups called guilds, each responsible for a different type of craft. Benin was particularly famous for its bronze artefacts and ivory carvings.

AMINA: WARRIOR QUEEN

Amina was born a princess in 1533 in Zazzau (now Nigeria). In 1549 she became the heir apparent to her mother. With the title came responsibility for a ward in the city where she arranged daily councils with other officials. She also began training in the cavalry. In 1576 Amina became the undisputed ruler of Zazzau. Distinguished as a soldier and an empire builder, she led military campaigns within months of becoming ruler. She built walled forts as area garrisons to combine the territory conquered after each campaign. Some of these forts still stand today. During her rule, Amina conquered the whole area between Zazzau and the Niger and Benue rivers. Amina's achievement was the closest any ruler had come to bringing the region now known as Nigeria under a single authority before British rule.

Queen Amina is remembered and celebrated on this Nigerian stamp.

MUNHUMUTAPA

The empire of Munhumutapa dominated the south African region that we now know as the countries of Zimbabwe, Mozambique and South Africa. The empire controlled the region from the 12th or 13th century until it was conquered by Portugal in 1629.

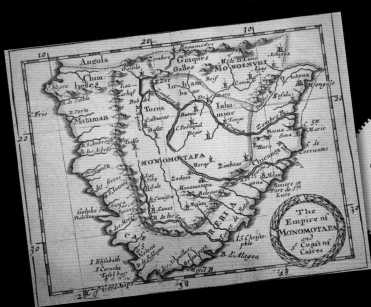

A Portuguese map of the Munhumutapa Empire shows its vast spread.

SPRAWLING EMPIRE

Spreading from the Zimbabwe region into South Africa and Mozambique, Munhumutapa (or Monomotapa as the Portuguese called it) grew wealthy by producing iron, copper and gold. It is believed to have been founded by Mutota, king of the Shona people from Zimbabwe. He travelled inland with the aim of conquering the land between the Zambezi and Limpopo rivers and the coast. A later ruler, Matope, conquered more territory and the Munhumutapa Empire grew. It was defended by a strong, well-trained army.

By the 16th century, Munhumutapa was working with Portugal to trade ivory and gold along the East African coast. The Portuguese had a bigger prize in mind, however. In 1629 they forced the local ruler to sign a treaty that made the empire a vassal state of Portugal.

GREAT ZIMBABWE

The cultural capital of Munhumutapa was Great Zimbabwe. It was a complex, consisting of 12 buildings spread over several square kilometres. Included was a hilltop castle that overlooked the entire area. Although now perished, thatched cottages also existed all over Great Zimbabwe. It is thought that around 25,000 people lived there in the 14th century. This would make the city slightly larger than medieval London, which had a population of around 20,000.

Great Zimbabwe is just one of 600 ruins dotted over the regions of Zimbabwe, Mozambique and South Africa. Archaeologists have studied stone ruins as far south as Johannesburg, as far east as the Mozambique coast and as far north as Zambia. The scope of the ruins indicates the great spread of the Munhumutapa Empire.

TOP TRADERS

Munhumutapa's trade had a long reach. During archaeological excavations, porcelain from China and glass beads from India have been discovered there.

This golden model of a rhinoceros was found at Mapungubwe in South Africa.

UNCOVERING MUTAPA

At the site of Mapungubwe, on the northern border of South Africa, archaeologists have uncovered a wealth of remains of the Munhumutapa Empire. These include golden artefacts, including a small model of a rhinoceros and a sceptre. In medieval times, the southern Africans mined an astonishing 43 million tons of gold ore. From this, they produced 700 tons of pure gold. At today's gold prices, this would have been worth around £20 billion.

A 17th century print of an emperor of Munhumutapa.

THE EAST AFRICAN COAST

Along the East African coast was the Swahili Confederation. Founded around CE 700, this union of neighbouring countries reached great prosperity in the 13th century, largely thanks to its success at trading across the Indian Ocean.

CITIES AND BUILDING

The great Swahili cities included Mogadishu on the Somali coast, Gedi on the Kenyan coast, the island of Zanzibar and the city-state of Kilwa, both off the Tanzanian coast. The Swahilis had a high standard of architecture. A typical East African front door had a central piece, brass pulls and wooden floral designs. The houses were between one and five storeys tall with exquisite wall designs, bathrooms, toilets and drains.

TRADE GIANTS

Steel was the main product the East Africans shipped across the neighbouring Indian Ocean. In 1978, archaeologists uncovered 13 ancient steel furnaces in Tanzania. These smelters made the finest steel found anywhere in the world before the mid-19th century. The Swahilis also minted their own coins of copper and silver. Thanks to trade, archaeologists discovered some 11th century Swahili coins as far away as northern Australia.

The East African coastline, showing the cities of Mogadishu and Kilwa.

Socotra Is.

Tana R.

Mogadishu
Gezira
Brava

Ungwanna

Manda
Malindi
Mombasa

Zanzibar Is.

INDIAN OCEAN

Mafia Is.
Kilwa Is.

Rufiji R.

Comoro Is.

Zambezi R. • Tete
Sinna •

MADAGASCAR

Sofala •

QVILOA

The city of Kilwa was located on an island off the coast of Tanzania. It was described as one of the most beautiful cities in the world.

These copper coins were minted in the Swahili Confederation.

Kilwa's Great Mosque is the largest surviving Swahili temple, founded in the 10th or 11th century.

MEET THE PEOPLE

Ibn Battuta, a Moroccan visitor to East Africa in 1331, wrote of his travels. He described the Somalis as black and the Tanzanians as extremely black with tattoo marks cut into their faces.

SWAHILI

Swahili emerged as the language of trade along the East African coast and became one of the African languages with the most highly developed literature. Four thousand old manuscripts can be found in the University of Dar es Salaam in Tanzania. Over 600 manuscripts are found in Zanzibari collections. Other Swahili manuscripts are in collections in Germany and London. Many Swahili epic poems are more than 5,000 quatrains long.

FOREIGN INVADERS

The Swahili Confederation declined after the Portuguese attempted to colonise the region in the early 16th century, during the early period of the slave trade (see p.28–38). They burned its cities, including Kilwa, which was left in ruins. Later destruction and more enslavement came from the Arabs who dominated the East African coast after 1698.

THE TRANSATLANTIC SLAVE TRADE BEGINS

In 1441 Portuguese sailors led raids along the African coast, kidnapping twelve Africans from Morocco. On their return, the sailors offered the captives to Prince Henry of Portugal.

From these small beginnings, the raid started a historical chapter of global importance. Europeans would dominate and enslave Africans for the next 400 years. Europeans would also conquer the Americas and carry out the genocide of its indigenous peoples.

FORGIVEN BY THE POPE

Portugal quickly recognised the potential of slavery for supplying manpower. Prince Henry sent word to Pope Eugene IV of his plans for more conquests and enslavement in Africa. The Pope offered to grant "... to all of those who shall be engaged in the said war, complete forgiveness of all their sins." The Portuguese thus saw themselves as exonerated of any wrongdoing.

In 1482 the Portuguese built Elmina Castle in Ghana – the first of many dungeons built along the West African coast to hold captured Africans.

This Benin bronze sculpture from the 17th century depicts the increasingly common sight of armed Portuguese soldiers in Africa.

This illustration shows Spanish soldiers capturing and killing defenceless Native Americans during their conquest of the Americas.

NIGRITÆ OB HISPANORVM CRVDELITATEM FVGI IIII
unt, aliquot Hifpanos cædunt, fed tandem ab Hifpanis va-
rijs fupplicijs adficiuntur.

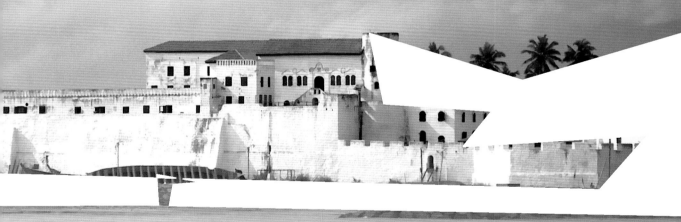

THE AMERICAS

At first, enslaved Africans were transported to Europe or islands off the coast of Africa. After Christopher Columbus arrived in the Americas in 1492 from Spain, the Spanish began the wars against the Native Americans, killing or enslaving them and seizing their lands. The Spanish and Portuguese conquerors soon needed workers for their new colonies in Central America and the islands of the Caribbean. Initially they only enslaved Native Americans, but too many died, lacking immunity to diseases transported by the Europeans. This created a need for workers from elsewhere, and so captured Africans were now shipped directly to the Americas to work.

SLAVES IN PORTUGAL

By the early 16th century, around 10 per cent of the population of Lisbon, Portugal's capital, was of African descent.

A TRADE IN HUMAN MISERY

By the 17th century, the shipping powerhouses of Holland, England and France had entered the slave trade, taking over from the Portuguese and the Spanish. They, too, slaughtered Native Americans and Caribbean islanders and seized their land. They too, shipped African captives across the sea to supply cheap labour for their colonies in the Caribbean and North America.

A TRIANGULAR TRADE

The slave trade developed into a well-travelled and lucrative route, linking Europe, Africa and the Americas in a triangular journey. From Africa, captured Africans were shipped directly across the Atlantic to the Americas via what was known as the Middle Passage. From the Americas, enslaved Africans produced foods, such as sugar and rice, and products, such as tobacco, that were shipped on to Europe. Finally, from Europe, manufactured goods including cloth, iron products, alcohol and firearms were exported for sale to enslavers in Africa.

This map shows the triangular route taken by ships during the slave trade.

Enslaved Africans were shackled together with thick chains during their journey.

THE MIDDLE PASSAGE

The journey to the Americas through the Middle Passage for enslaved Africans was extremely harsh. Captives on the slave ships were typically 13 or 14 years old. Some were much younger, others, much older. All were kept below deck in horrible conditions where disease spread rapidly. If an enslaved African showed evidence of yellow fever, dysentery, measles or small pox, they were thrown overboard to prevent the spread of these illnesses. Only around 80 per cent of people who began the fifty-day journey arrived alive.

AUCTIONS

Those Africans that arrived alive in the Americas and the Caribbean were sold at public auctions. The enslavers washed, deloused and oiled the skin of their captives to improve their appearance and make them look healthy and strong. On the auction blocks, potential buyers inspected the captives, checking for signs of disease before making their choice. Young, fit Africans were worth the most money. Once bought, the new owner burned a hot iron with a logo on it into the African's skin. Called branding, this left a permanent mark of ownership. Following this, the owner gave the African a European name. They were not allowed to use their original names and were forced to follow their owner's religion.

OLAUDAH EQUIANO

One captured African, Olaudah Equiano (c.1745–1797), was renamed Gustavus Vassa. In his autobiography *The Interesting Life of Olaudah Equiano* he recalled the emotional impact of being auctioned: "On a signal given ... the buyers rush at once into the yard where the slaves are confined, and make choice of that parcel they like best. The noise ... with which this is attended, and the eagerness visible in the countenances of the buyers, serve ... to increase the apprehensions of the terrified Africans ... In this manner ... are relations and friends separated, most of them never to see each other again. I remember in the vessel in which I was brought over ... there were several brothers, who, in the sale, were sold in different lots; and it was very moving ... to see and hear their cries at parting."

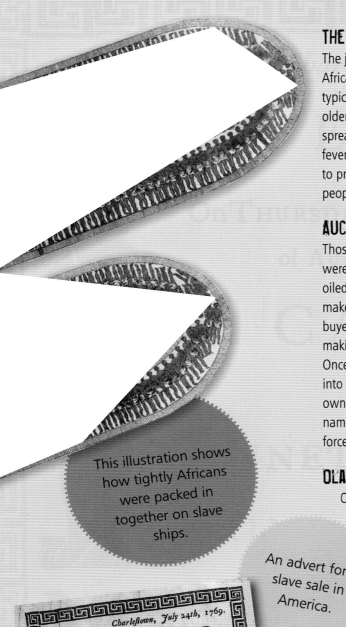

This illustration shows how tightly Africans were packed in together on slave ships.

An advert for a slave sale in America.

COST OF LIFE
The average price paid for an enslaved African is estimated to have been around £20.

LIFE AS A SLAVE

Life for enslaved Africans in the colonies was very hard, with backbreaking work, no pay and no freedom.

SLAVE LABOUR

Slaves worked from sunrise to sunset, only breaking off at breakfast and lunchtime. Some workers dug precious metals and minerals from mines. Others cut sugarcane on plantations or sweated in sugar refineries. Many grew tobacco on farms or processed it in factories. Others laboured on building sites and as domestic servants. The work was gruelling and exhausting. The average life expectancy of plantation slaves was only around seven to nine years. Many captives died young and had to be replaced by other slaves.

OWNERS

Alongside their harsh work, enslaved Africans were subjected to cruel treatment by their owners, who largely viewed them as their property. As the people in power in the colonies were slave-owners themselves, there was little chance that slavers would be punished for mistreating their workers. Slaves were regularly whipped for any wrongdoing, while those who ran away but were later captured could be hanged or shot.

Slave-owners often shot any slaves who tried to run away.

MAROONS

The Maroons was a name given to Africans in the Americas and the Caribbean who escaped from slavery and built communities of their own. Many of them revived traditional African customs, languages and religions. Some Maroon communities remained independent from European rule, having never been recaptured and enslaved. This was true of Maroons in Guyana, Surinam, Jamaica and Florida.

MINI-AFRICA

Palmares in northern Brazil was the most impressive of these mini-Africas. Beginning in 1595, a small band of enslaved Africans revolted against their Portuguese and Dutch masters and fled into the forests. Little by little, their numbers grew to a settlement of around 30,000. They created the first government of free Blacks in the Americas. Palmares flourished until 1694, when it fell to a Portuguese army. Palmares' leader Zumbi (1655–1695), a skilled warrior and Palmares' greatest king, was captured and killed.

RUN WILD
The name 'Maroon' is believed to come from the Spanish word *cimarrón*, meaning wild.

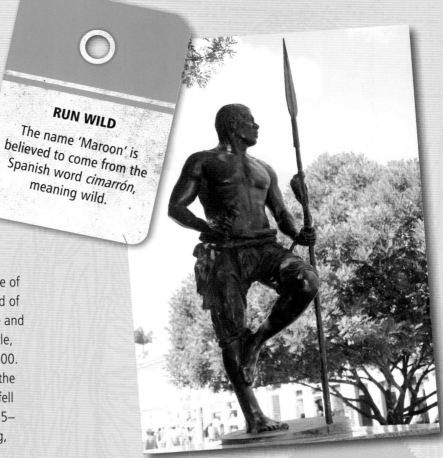

The memorial to Zumbi in Salvador, Brazil.

Black Consciousness Day is held every year in Brazil on 20 November – the date of Zumbi's death.

33

GROWING RESISTANCE

Throughout the slave trade, many enslaved Africans bravely took a stand against their treatment and the treatment of their fellow Africans, with actions both big and small.

SMALL ACTS

Many slaves used a campaign of passive resistance to frustrate their owners. This could include working very slowly, feigning illness and breaking tools or machinery. Other enslaved workers simply ran away, despite the risk of harsh punishment.

UPRISINGS

Some resistance was more active and violent. Some enslaved Africans led uprisings on the ship journey between Africa and the Americas. It is estimated that up to one in ten slave ships experienced some kind of rebellion. Famous examples include the Marlborough Revolt of 1753 where 420 Africans seized control of the Bristol ship and returned it to the West African coast, and the *Amistad* rebellion in 1839. Other enslaved Africans led organised revolts on plantations, such as the planned rebellion in Antigua in 1736. Such rebellions were very dangerous, not only for the workers. As the slaves greatly outnumbered their enslavers, the enslavers could not risk these rebellions gaining momentum and were quick to respond with harsh reprisals. In Antigua, for example, the plot was uncovered before it could be put into action and 88 Africans were killed, mostly by being burned alive.

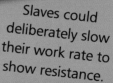

Slaves could deliberately slow their work rate to show resistance.

A scene from the 1997 film *Amistad*, which was directed by Stephen Spielberg.

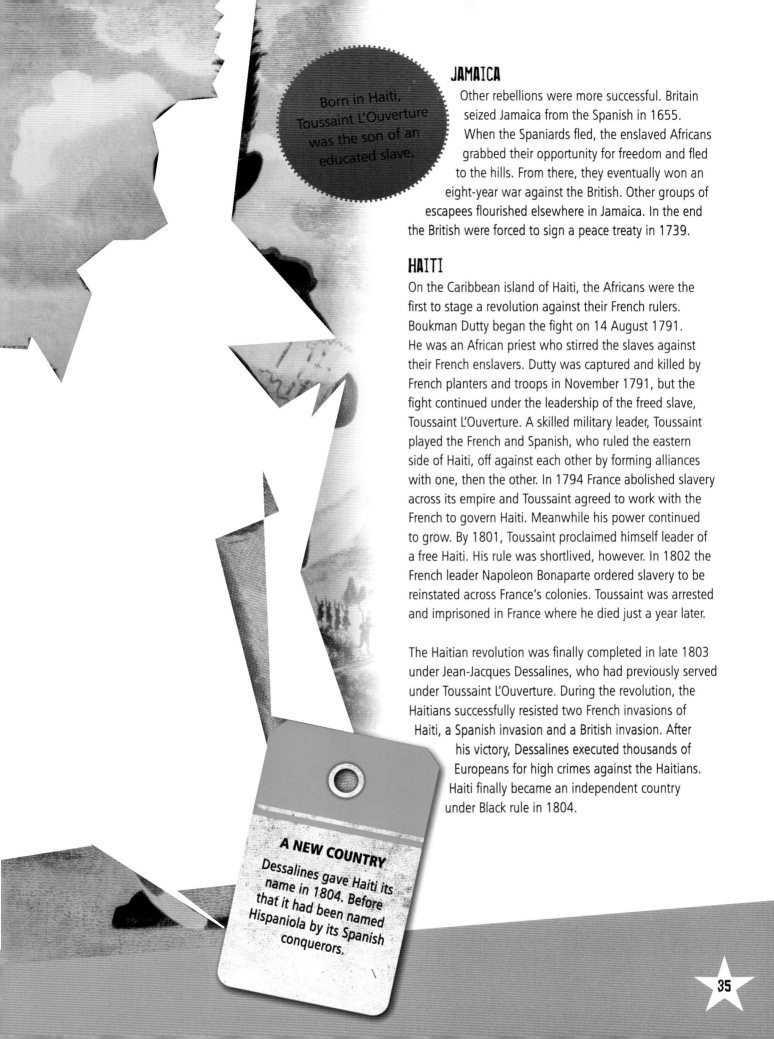

Born in Haiti, Toussaint L'Ouverture was the son of an educated slave.

JAMAICA

Other rebellions were more successful. Britain seized Jamaica from the Spanish in 1655. When the Spaniards fled, the enslaved Africans grabbed their opportunity for freedom and fled to the hills. From there, they eventually won an eight-year war against the British. Other groups of escapees flourished elsewhere in Jamaica. In the end the British were forced to sign a peace treaty in 1739.

HAITI

On the Caribbean island of Haiti, the Africans were the first to stage a revolution against their French rulers. Boukman Dutty began the fight on 14 August 1791. He was an African priest who stirred the slaves against their French enslavers. Dutty was captured and killed by French planters and troops in November 1791, but the fight continued under the leadership of the freed slave, Toussaint L'Ouverture. A skilled military leader, Toussaint played the French and Spanish, who ruled the eastern side of Haiti, off against each other by forming alliances with one, then the other. In 1794 France abolished slavery across its empire and Toussaint agreed to work with the French to govern Haiti. Meanwhile his power continued to grow. By 1801, Toussaint proclaimed himself leader of a free Haiti. His rule was shortlived, however. In 1802 the French leader Napoleon Bonaparte ordered slavery to be reinstated across France's colonies. Toussaint was arrested and imprisoned in France where he died just a year later.

The Haitian revolution was finally completed in late 1803 under Jean-Jacques Dessalines, who had previously served under Toussaint L'Ouverture. During the revolution, the Haitians successfully resisted two French invasions of Haiti, a Spanish invasion and a British invasion. After his victory, Dessalines executed thousands of Europeans for high crimes against the Haitians. Haiti finally became an independent country under Black rule in 1804.

A NEW COUNTRY

Dessalines gave Haiti its name in 1804. Before that it had been named Hispaniola by its Spanish conquerors.

ABOLITION

By the mid-18th century public opinion around the world was turning against the slave trade, and organisations were beginning to actively campaign against it.

PETITIONS AND BOYCOTTS

Among the earliest opponents of the slave trade was a religious group called the Quakers. Its members believed that all men were created equal and so no man should be able to own another. In Britain, the Society for the Abolition of the Slave Trade was formed in 1787. Its members included the freed slave and campaigner Olaudah Equiano (see page 31), reformers Granville Sharp, Elizabeth Heyrick and Thomas Clarkson, and the MP William Wilberforce. They wrote letters and petitions and toured Britain, drawing attention to the cruelty of the slave trade. They also organised a mass boycott of Caribbean sugar.

By 1791, the first abolition bill was proposed in Parliament by William Wilberforce, but it was defeated. He returned to Parliament with a new bill every year until the Slave Trade Abolition Bill was eventually passed in 1807.

Phillis Wheatley

Phillis Wheatley (c.1753–1784) was the first African-American published poet. Born in West Africa, she was sold into slavery at the age of seven and transported to North America. Her enslavers, the Wheatley family, taught her to read English, Latin and French. Rich with Biblical influences, Phillis published *Poems on Various Subjects, Religious and Moral* in 1773, bringing her fame both in America and Europe. Phillis was opposed to slavery and wrote many letters to ministers and others on the principles of freedom. She was emancipated and married John Peters, a free Black man, but sadly died in 1784 due to complications from childbirth.

This powerful woodcut was used by the Society for the Abolition of the Slave Trade to draw attention to the slaves' plight.

JAMAICA FIGHTS BACK

In practice, although the slave trade was banned in British colonies, slavery continued. In Jamaica in 1831, Sam Sharpe, a Baptist preacher, led 60,000 enslaved Africans in the biggest act of resistance so far. Initially peaceful, the revolt grew violent – plantations were destroyed and plantation-owners killed. The British army restored order and Sharpe was executed, but the revolt put further pressure on the British government to completely end the slave trade. They passed laws abolishing the enslavement of Africans in the British Empire in 1833, which came into effect in 1838. Freedom from slavery came to Africans in the French colonies in 1848, and in the Dutch colonies in 1863.

FREEDOM IN AMERICA

In the USA, slavery was abolished in some northern states as early as 1787, but it continued in the southern states, with millions of enslaved Africans working on the South's huge cotton plantations. It was a key factor in the American Civil War, which raged from 1861 to 1865. The northern states eventually won the brutal conflict and slavery was formally abolished across the USA in 1865.

UNDERCOVER AID

Some American slaves used the Underground Railroad to escape to freedom. This secret network of safe houses and secret routes was organised by abolitionists and former slaves. It is estimated that around 100,000 slaves were helped by the Underground Railroad.

People celebrating the abolition of slavery in the USA in Washington DC.

THE LEGACY OF THE SLAVE TRADE

In 1888 Brazil became the last country to legally abolish the transatlantic slave trade, ending over 400 years of human suffering, though slavery lives on in many forms today.

PAYING BACK

One condition of the 1833 Slavery Abolition Act (see p.37) was that the British government agreed to pay slave-owners reparations for the loss of their workers. However, no African nation has yet received any compensation for the loss of their people.

WARRING CONTINENT

Within Africa, slavery created huge divisions. Most slaves were captured from central and western African countries where their leaders thought it was better to betray their neighbours than be enslaved themselves. Consequently, nations raided each other in horrific wars that were often part-funded by the European slavers themselves. They sold their captured rivals to enslavers to buy weapons with which they hoped to protect themselves from being raided. For refugees from these wars, trying to find places of safety was of utmost urgency. Some found refuge only in swamps, on the hills or in remote caves. Other Africans were simply captured from their villages by raiding parties, organised by the European enslavers.

The scene as Nigerian soldiers raid a village in search of slaves

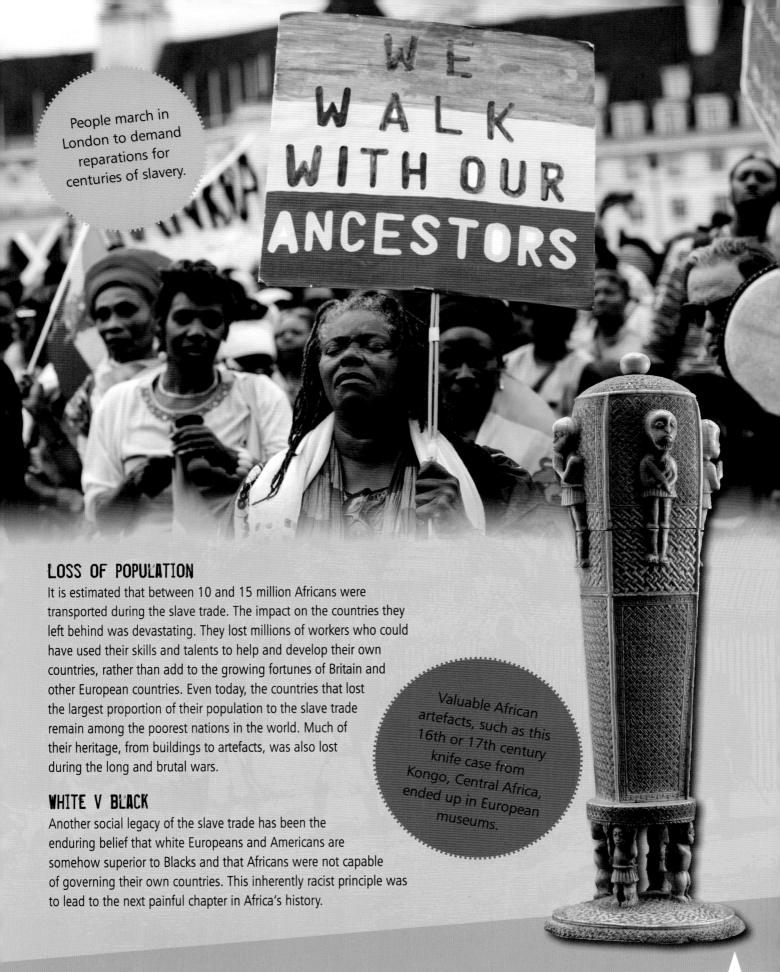

People march in London to demand reparations for centuries of slavery.

WE WALK WITH OUR ANCESTORS

Valuable African artefacts, such as this 16th or 17th century knife case from Kongo, Central Africa, ended up in European museums.

LOSS OF POPULATION

It is estimated that between 10 and 15 million Africans were transported during the slave trade. The impact on the countries they left behind was devastating. They lost millions of workers who could have used their skills and talents to help and develop their own countries, rather than add to the growing fortunes of Britain and other European countries. Even today, the countries that lost the largest proportion of their population to the slave trade remain among the poorest nations in the world. Much of their heritage, from buildings to artefacts, was also lost during the long and brutal wars.

WHITE V BLACK

Another social legacy of the slave trade has been the enduring belief that white Europeans and Americans are somehow superior to Blacks and that Africans were not capable of governing their own countries. This inherently racist principle was to lead to the next painful chapter in Africa's history.

THE SCRAMBLE FOR AFRICA

Towards the end of the 19th century, with no real opportunity to recover from the slave trade, Africa faced a second onslaught from Europe: the era of colonialism.

DIVIDING UP AFRICA

During a conference in Berlin, Germany, held in 1884–1885, known as the Congo or Berlin Conference, some European nations, including Great Britain, France, Portugal, Belgium and Germany, agreed to effectively occupy Africa. They saw it as an opportunity to colonise Africans, seize Africa's rich resources, including minerals, oil and timber and, moreover, seize African lands to prevent their European rivals from taking them. *The Times* newspaper at the time called it the 'Scramble for Africa'.

FIGHTING BACK

Some African rulers led their people to battle the invading Europeans to resist being colonised. Among these were the Mahdi in Sudan, the 'Mad Mullah' in Somalia, Behanzin in Dahomey (today's Benin and Togo), Queen Mother Yaa Asentewa in the Ashanti Empire (Ghana), Lobenguela in Matabeleland (Zimbabwe) and Cetewayo in the Zulu Empire (South Africa). One famous African victory was the Zulu triumph over British invaders at Isandlwana in 1879. The celebrations here and elsewhere were short-lived, however. All these lands were overrun by Europeans in the end.

The Berlin conference of 1884–1885 laid the basis for the European colonisation of Africa.

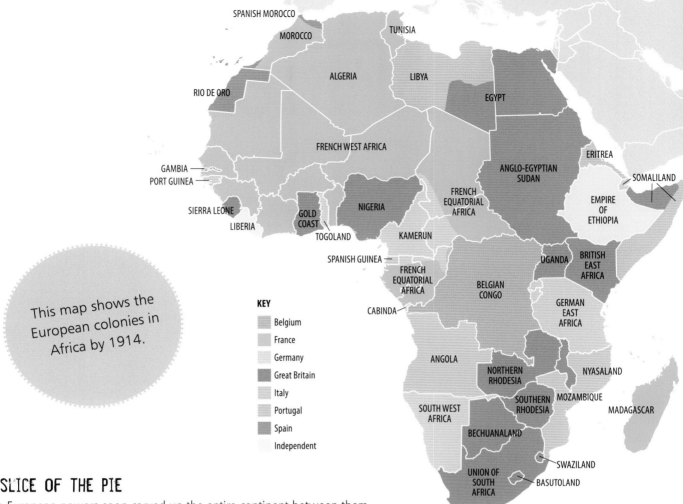

KEY

Belgium
France
Germany
Great Britain
Italy
Portugal
Spain
Independent

This map shows the European colonies in Africa by 1914.

A SLICE OF THE PIE

The European powers soon carved up the entire continent between them. By the outbreak of the First World War in 1914, 90 per cent of African territory was under European control. Only Ethiopia and Liberia remained independent. Great Britain took the greatest amount of territory, comprising nearly 30 per cent of Africa's population, with huge colonies scattered across the continent. France seized enormous swathes of West Africa, while Portugal and Germany took control of selected lands to the far east and west of Africa. Belgium ruled over a large area of central Africa, which became known as the Congo Free State (later the Belgian Congo).

FOREIGN RULE

The European colonisers established the new borders for African countries, paying no attention to local or cultural identity, and made their own languages the official languages of the countries. The Africans themselves had no say in these matters. The Europeans used extreme brutality to seize and rule the conquered lands. They instituted genocide and 'forced labour' – a polite term for slavery. It is estimated that as many as 11 million Africans disappeared between 1885 and 1908 when King Leopold of Belgium ruled the Congo Free State.

This cartoon shows King Leopold of Belgium protecting his money made from the Congo Free State, while the Congolese suffer.

41

THE PAN-AFRICAN CONGRESSES

By the early 20th century, Black people were at their lowest political position ever. Africans everywhere were ruled by Europeans. The Caribbean was ruled by Europe. Blacks in the USA were segregated and could legally be treated as second-class citizens. Only Haiti and Ethiopia remained truly free.

THE COLOUR LINE

In 1900 Henry Sylvester Williams, a Trinidadian lawyer and one of the founders of the African Association, called the first Pan-African Conference in London. At the conference, Dr William Du Bois, an African-American scholar, predicted that the central problem of the 20th century was going to be 'the problem of the colour line'. Thus, the Pan African Movement began as a small number of Black intellectuals outside Africa. They came together to strategise a response to global European domination. Following the conference, Williams set up branches of the Pan-African Association in Jamaica, Trinidad and the USA.

EARLY CONGRESSES

Dr Du Bois went on to lead the first Pan-African Congress in Paris in 1919. At the Congress, the delegates asked the European colonial powers to protect the Africans that they ruled. At the Second Pan-African Congress, held in London and Brussels in 1921, the delegates went further to ask that Africans be allowed local self-government. At the Third Pan-African Congress in London and Lisbon in 1923, they asked that 'Black folk be treated as men'. The Fourth Pan-African Congress in New York in 1927 was the last one led directly by Dr Du Bois.

PAN-AFRICAN CONFERENCE.

WESTMINSTER TOWN HALL,

ON THE

23rd, 24th and 25th JULY, 1900.

This Conference is organised by a Committee of the African Association for the Discussion of the "Native Races" Question, and will be attended and addressed by those of African descent from all parts of the British Empire, the United States of America, Abyssinia, Liberia, Hayti, etc.

YOU ARE CORDIALLY AND EARNESTLY INVITED TO ATTEND.

CONFERENCES—Morning, 10.30 and Evening,

H. S. WILLIAMS, *Hon. Sec.*,
139, PALACE CHAMBERS, S.

An invitation to the first Pan-African Conference in 1900.

The author and activist Dr William Du Bois in 1919.

MARCUS GARVEY

The Honourable Marcus Garvey, Du Bois' rival, tried different methods to get rights for Black people. Born in Jamaica into a Maroon family, in 1914 he founded the Universal Negro Improvement Association and African Communities League (UNIA) in Jamaica. In 1920 Garvey led the UNIA at its first convention in New York, where he now lived. Garvey urged Black people to take pride in their African heritage and support freeing Africa from European rule to build a powerful base in Africa. A powerful Africa could then defend Black people all over the globe. The association soon had over 1,100 branches in more than 40 countries, including Cuba, Costa Rica, Venezuela, Ghana, Liberia and South Africa. At one point it was estimated to have over six million members.

The celebrated Black nationalist, Marcus Garvey, in 1920.

THE UNIA

Under Garvey the UNIA set up its own industries, including factories, shops and restaurants, and a weekly newspaper called the *Negro World*. It also established two steamship companies to transport returning Blacks to Africa. But in 1923 Garvey was arrested for fraud, sent to prison and later deported. It has been suggested that his arrest was politically motivated at the request of the US government.

THE FIFTH PAN-AFRICAN CONGRESS

Eventually, Garvey's first wife, Amy Ashwood Garvey, the journalist and activist George Padmore and an ageing Dr Du Bois, among others, organised the Fifth Pan-African Congress in Manchester, England, in 1945. For the first time, Africans directly from Africa were in large numbers at the event, including future African leaders Kwame Nkrumah and Jomo Kenyatta (see p.44–45). More importantly, for the first time the Congress called for African independence.

Delegates at the Fifth Pan-African Congress in Manchester in 1945.

AN INDEPENDENT AFRICA

When it finally arrived, African independence was relatively swift and brutal.

THE ATLANTIC CHARTER

In 1941, in the midst of the Second World War (1939–1945), the US President Franklin D Roosevelt and Sir Winston Churchill, the prime minister of the UK, met to discuss their common goals from the conflict. From their discussions, among other things, was agreed the Atlantic Charter, which stated that the imperial colonies should be allowed to choose their own government. Churchill was opposed to the idea, but as the end of the war left many European powers, particularly the losing ones, poorer and stripped of power, independence from colonial rule became a much more real possibility.

INSPIRING OTHERS

The drive for African independence was partly inspired by the work of the activist Mahatma Gandhi (1869–1948) who helped lead India to independence from British rule in 1947.

Churchill (left) and Roosevelt agree the Atlantic Charter on board the battleship HMS *Prince of Wales*.

NEW LEADERS

By the late 1940s, independence movements were strengthening in many African countries, led by often western-educated African nationalists, such as Kwame Nkrumah (Ghana) and Jomo Kenyatta (Kenya) who saw how colonisation drained their countries' wealth and resources and boosted those of their colonisers.

INDEPENDENCE AT LAST

In 1957 Ghana became the first sub-Saharan African country to declare its independence. Other countries quickly followed – in 1960 17 African nations became independent, including Nigeria, the Ivory Coast and the Democratic Republic of Congo. Some nations' transitions were reasonably smooth. Others, however, such as Algeria's, resulted in a bitter eight-year war between France and the Algerian Front de Libération Nationale, during which hundreds of thousands of people died.

President Kwame Nkrumah, centre, leads the celebrations as Ghana becomes independent of British rule in 1957.

IMPOVERISHED AND DIVIDED

All these independent countries faced serious problems. Africans entered the independence period the poorest people on Earth, as the colonial powers had stripped them of much of their wealth, beginning with the slave trade and continuing with the colonial period. They were also among the most culturally divided, as the borders drawn up by the colonial powers forced together peoples who were traditionally separate, and divided others that belonged together. The new country of Nigeria, for example, included hundreds of historically separate cultures. All had also had foreign languages and learning forced upon them.

Frantz Fanon

Frantz Fanon (1925-1961) came from the Caribbean island of Martinique. He studied medicine and psychiatry in France. He also worked with French and Algerian soldiers in Algeria in the 1950s where he observed the impact of colonialism on people's minds. His first major book, *Black Skins, White Masks*, was the first to look at how the powers of Europe manipulated the thinking and emotions of the people they conquered. Fanon died aged just 35 of cancer.

SOUTHERN AFRICA
AND APARTHEID

While the rest of Africa embraced independence, despite its many challenges, one part of the continent initially rejected it: southern Africa.

PORTUGAL RESISTS

In the 1960s, Mozambique and Angola in southern Africa, and the smaller countries of Guinea-Bissau, São Tomé and Príncipe and Cape Verde in West Africa, remained colonies of Portugal. Portugal, ruled by Prime Minister António de Oliveira Salazar, was opposed to independence, still seeing the colonies as part of the Portuguese Empire. But nationalism was building in these countries, leading to 14 years of uprisings and armed confrontation, during which hundreds of thousands of people died or became refugees. In 1974, in the so-called Carnation Revolution, Portugal's government was overthrown and it soon after withdrew from all its African colonies.

When Africans in Rhodesia defeated the British colonisers, they renamed the country Zimbabwe.

ZIMBABWE

The British white rulers in Zimbabwe, then called Rhodesia, also resisted change. The people of Zimbabwe waged a military struggle, led by two major rival liberation organisations – ZANU, headed by Robert Mugabe, and ZAPU, under Joshua Nkomo. After years of bitter fighting, ZANU eventually won a landslide electoral victory. Robert Mugabe became prime minister of the newly renamed Zimbabwe in April 1980.

Blacks and whites in South Africa were strictly divided. This sign tells visitors this area of beach is reserved for whites.

THE DIVISIONAL COUNCIL OF THE CAPE
WHITE AREA
BY ORDER SECRETARY
DIE AFDELINGSRAAD VAN DIE KAAP
OP LAS SEKRETARIS

Nelson Mandela greets crowds during his election campaign in 1994.

APARTHEID

The biggest obstacle to Black freedom came from the apartheid state in South Africa and neighbouring Namibia, which was then under South African rule. Moreover, South Africa and its government had many supporters in the United States, Great Britain and Israel. Racial segregation was in place all over Africa under colonialism, but it became much stricter in South Africa after the 1948 election was won by the National Party, which promoted white supremacy and racial segregation. Apartheid divided South Africans by their colour and forced each group to live apart from each other at work, at home and in schools. Meanwhile a number of Land Acts were passed by the South African government that awarded more than 80 per cent of farmland to whites, ensuring that the minority whites remained at the top of society, and the majority Blacks at the bottom of society.

A RAINBOW NATION

Apartheid remained in place for over thirty years. Eventually, following growing international pressure on South Africa, including economic sanctions, the last white president F. W. de Klerk abolished apartheid. Following the first all-race national elections, activist-turned-leader Nelson Mandela became the first Black president of South Africa in 1994. Mandela and de Klerk were awarded the Nobel Peace Prize for their efforts to change South Africa from white minority rule to Black majority rule without bloodshed.

"We have, at last, achieved our political emancipation [....]
We shall build the society in which all South Africans, both Black and white, will be able to walk tall, without any fear in their hearts, assured of their inalienable right to human dignity – a rainbow nation at peace with itself and the world."

Nelson Mandela

AFRICAN-AMERICANS IN THE USA

While slavery ended in the USA in 1865, it did not lead to real equality for African-Americans for many years.

SEPARATE SEATING

The separation of whites and Blacks in the US had continued long after the Civil War, particularly in the southern states. In 1896, one generation after the end of slavery, the US Supreme Court heard the case of a mixed-race African-American man, Homer Plessy, who argued that he should be allowed to sit in a train carriage reserved for white passengers. His appeal was rejected, and segregation was ruled to be constitutional by the Supreme Court.

JIM CROW LAWS

Segregation was enforced by the so-called Jim Crow Laws, which in theory offered Blacks and whites a 'separate but equal' life. This created all-white districts where Black people could not live. There were all-white schools and universities that Black people could not attend. The majority of African-Americans were not allowed to vote in political elections. Even parks, toilets, waiting rooms and prisons were strictly segregated.

PLAYING BLACK
The Jim Crow laws were named after a foolish Black character called Jim Crow. He was played by a white actor who blackened his face for the role.

A Ku Klux Klan member dangles a noose out of his car as a grim nod to lynchings.

LIVING IN FEAR

While segregation continued through the late 19th and early 20th century, racial discrimination continued too, and tensions grew between Black and white people. Groups such as the Ku Klux Klan, a white supremacist organisation, fed on this unease and flourished. African-Americans, particularly those living in the southern states, faced the constant threat of violence at the hands of unauthorised 'lynch' mobs of men. These mobs would seize a man who had been accused of a crime – often sexual assault of a white woman – torture and hang them, without any trial.

THE NAACP

The National Association for the Advancement of Colored People (NAACP) was founded in 1909 to fight for the rights of African-Americans. It included both African-Americans, such as Dr William Du Bois (see p.42–43) and journalist Ida B Wells, and whites, including social activists Mary White Ovington and Henry Moskowitz. One of its early campaigns took on lynching and in 1917 around 10,000 people took part in a march against the practice in New York. The NAACP went on to play a major part in the advancement of African-American civil rights through peaceful protest and government lobbying.

This photo, taken at a barbecue in the USA, clearly shows segregation in action.

THE FIGHT FOR CIVIL RIGHTS

The Black civil rights movement in the USA grew in momentum throughout the 20th century, championed by diverse and powerful leaders.

TEACHER AND LEADER

Booker T Washington was a prominent African-American leader. Growing up in a poor family, he started working at the age of nine but later attended school, where he worked as a janitor to pay his way. Washington became a teacher and in 1881 he founded the Tuskegee Institute in Alabama, which became the foremost Black university. He believed that African-Americans should embrace business education, mechanics and agriculture. He wanted to build a Black business class by getting Black people to help and support each other and later formed the National Negro Business League to help achieve this aim. As his renown grew, Washington became a popular and powerful speaker on Black rights.

Booker T Washington on stage in the Black community of Mound Bayou in Mississippi in 1912.

THE NATION OF ISLAM

Activist Marcus Garvey (see p.43) read Washington's 1901 autobiography *Up From Slavery* and was inspired by its message of empowerment and self-help, which guided him to found the UNIA in 1914. Elijah Muhammad joined the UNIA in the 1920s. However, as the movement began to lose its power following Garvey's deportation in 1927, Muhammad decided to start his own movement. In 1934, he became the Supreme Minister of the Nation of Islam, a political and religious group that aimed to create an all-Black country based on Islam by taking total control of the south-east portion of the United States. Islam was, of course, a dominant religion in Africa just before the slave trade. In 1951, Muhammad found a young minister who was magnetic enough to draw thousands of people to his movement: Malcolm X (see p.52).

INSPIRATIONAL PREACHER

Baptist minister and activist Dr Martin Luther King had a different view. Unlike Muhammad, Garvey and Washington, King wanted Black people to participate in American society and not to live a separate existence. Consequently, he believed that Blacks should fight to get the right to vote, fight for integration, fight against segregated schools and fight against discriminatory employment practices.

Elijah Muhammad addresses a Nation of Islam convention. The boxer Muhammad Ali can be seen to his right.

Duke Ellington

Despite many years of segregation, Black people all over the USA made significant cultural contributions to their country. Duke Ellington (1899–1974) was one of the most important composers in American history. Through jazz, he demonstrated that Blacks could create music equal in intellect to the best minds.

Creating his first masterpieces in 1927 like 'Creole Love Call' and 'The Blues I Love to Sing', Ellington mastered the three-minute form. He used his orchestra in revolutionary ways, creating new sounds never heard before in any form of music. His 1934 'Symphony In Black' took the listener on a musical roller coaster through a work scene, unreciprocated love and a funeral scene. 'A Tone Parallel to Harlem', 1951, uses the jazz language with all the skill and complexity of a classical overture to paint scenes in the life of Harlem, New York.

51

CHANGE AT LAST

Black civil rights leaders used different methods to broadcast their message to the people. Eventually, their voices were heard across the USA and the world.

PEACEFUL PROTEST

Dr Martin Luther King led marches, boycotts and other peaceful demonstrations against the poor treatment of African-Americans, beginning with the Birmingham bus boycott of 1955–56 where thousands protested against racial segregation on buses. Dr King soon attracted the attention of the world media, culminating in his march on Washington DC on 28 August 1963. Here, over 200,000 people came together to hear Dr King famously declare his dream that one day, race would no longer keep people apart.

BLACK POWER

Malcolm X had a troubled youth and spent time in prison before joining the Nation of Islam. In contrast to Dr King, he urged his supporters to defend themselves, and advanced the idea of Black Power – believing that Black people should celebrate their heritage, rather than just become part of a white society. In 1964, Malcolm X split with the Nation of Islam to found the Muslim Mosque Inc.

BLACK FIGHTBACK

The Black Panthers rose during the late 1960s. Initially formed to protect African-Americans from police brutality, the Panthers became involved in armed battles with the law, leading then FBI director J Edgar Hoover to label them an enemy of the state. However, many of their policies were aimed at improving social welfare for African-Americans, including better education, housing and healthcare.

52

Barack Obama and his family celebrate his historic election as US president.

PROGRESS

Dr King and Malcolm X's work achieved important successes. In 1964 the American government conceded that segregation was wrong. The following year, they granted all African-Americans the right to vote. Tragically, both men met early and violent deaths. Malcolm X was shot dead in February 1965 by three members of the Nation of Islam. Dr King was assassinated in April 1968 by career criminal James Earl Ray.

JESSE JACKSON

Jesse Jackson, a Baptist minister and disciple of Dr King, continued to work for the advancement of Black people alongside the US Democratic Party. They supported policies that encouraged employers to hire a fair ratio of Black people, helping to grow the Black middle class. Jesse Jackson even ran for US president in 1984, but he was unsuccessful.

BARACK OBAMA

On 4 November 2008, Barack Obama, a Democratic senator of Kenyan and European heritage, became the 44th president of the USA. His election became a source of pride for Black people all over the world. In his victory speech Obama declared: "It's been a long time coming, but tonight ... change has come to America."

Oprah Winfrey at the 2018 Golden Globes Awards ceremony.

Oprah Winfrey

Oprah Winfrey (1954–) is an African-American actress, TV personality, entrepreneur and self-made billionaire. Growing up in rural poverty, Oprah has risen to become one of the most influential women in the world and uses her fame to campaign for the less fortunate, particularly in the field of education. At the 2018 Golden Globes, Oprah's impassioned speech in support of the #MeToo movement led people to speculate that she might one day run as the first female African-American president of the USA.

THE WINDRUSH GENERATION

Modern Black Britain began on 22 June 1948 when nearly 500 Caribbeans arrived at Tilbury Docks in Essex. They arrived from Jamaica on a ship called the *Empire Windrush*. They came with the excitement of starting a new life.

COMING HOME

Thousands of Caribbeans had served the United Kingdom in the armed forces during the Second World War as their home islands were then part of the British Empire. At the time, Caribbean people saw England as the 'Mother Country'. When the *Empire Windrush* called at Jamaica en route to the UK to pick up servicemen on leave from their units, hundreds of men, women and children decided to make the historic voyage.

The arrival of the *Empire Windrush* in 1948 was a turning point for Black culture in the UK.

WORKERS WANTED

In 1948, the UK was slowly recovering from the economic hardship of the Second World War. Workers were needed to help rebuild its services and industries, so the government passed the British Nationality Act, which officially recognised the citizenship of people from the UK and its colonies. In 1956 London Transport began recruiting workers from Barbados to work on the buses and the underground. Other recruitment programmes brought people to work for British Rail and the National Health Service.

Black postal service workers sort post at a London sorting office.

EMPIRE

LO

HOSTILE ENVIRONMENT

The Black arrivals often encountered hostility when they attempted to find homes and work. Many whites objected to Blacks moving into what they saw as 'their' areas and taking 'their' jobs. Many white landlords even refused to rent property to Blacks. They placed adverts that read: 'No Blacks, No Irish, No dogs.' Threats came from the Teddy Boys, a tough working-class white group, who led violent riots against Blacks in Notting Hill, west London, in the hot summer of 1958. They even killed an innocent Black man, Kelso Cochrane, in 1959.

FIGHTING BACK

Journalist and activist Claudia Jones emerged as the leader of the Black civil rights movement in the UK. In 1958, she founded the *West Indian Gazette* – the only newspaper for the Black community. The paper campaigned against anti-Black racism in housing, education and employment. Jones also launched the first Caribbean Carnival at St Pancras Hall in London, in 1959. Carnival highlighted Black culture. It was also designed to bring Black and white people together. Carnival moved to Notting Hill in the mid-1960s and has since evolved into one of the biggest street parties in the world.

The first Notting Hill Carnival in 1959 was a celebration of Caribbean culture.

CONTROVERSY

In May 2018, the UK government was engulfed in scandal when it was discovered that many thousands of Commonwealth citizens who arrived in the UK in the years following *Windrush* had been wrongly made redundant, denied healthcare and even threatened with deportation as they did not always have the paperwork to prove their right to live in the UK.

WINDRUSH
ON

BEING BLACK IN THE UK

Encouraged by civil rights progress in the USA, the demand for equal rights in the UK strengthened from the 1960s.

BUS BOYCOTT

Employers refusing to hire Blacks (known as the 'Colour Bar') remained a huge problem. In the UK's first Black-led campaign, Paul Stephenson, a youth worker, led the Bristol Bus Boycott of 1963. At the time, the Bristol Bus Company refused to employ Black or Asian drivers or conductors. Stephenson, inspired by Dr Martin Luther King (see p.52), called on people to boycott the bus company in protest. The boycott went on for four months, and attracted much public support, including that of UK Prime Minister Harold Wilson. In the end, the Bristol Bus Company agreed to hire Blacks and Asians.

The attention the boycott drew pushed the UK Parliament to pass the Race Relations Act of 1965. The first piece of legislation to tackle racism in the UK, it banned discrimination on the grounds of colour, race or ethnic or national origins in public places.

Paul Stephenson campaigning in Bristol in 1963.

JOCELYN BARROW

Teacher and activist Dame Jocelyn Barrow also challenged the Colour Bar. She helped set up the Campaign Against Racial Discrimination in 1965 to lobby Parliament to tackle racism, and was rewarded in 1968 when Parliament passed a second Race Relations Act, making it illegal to refuse housing, employment, or public services to a person on the grounds of colour, race, ethnic or national origins. Barrow continued to campaign for Black rights, in particular promoting the benefits of a multi-cultural education. She later became the first Black female governor of the BBC.

FRONT OF HOUSE

Among Barrow's achievements was persuading shop owners in Oxford Street to allow Blacks to serve customers. It was previously believed that white people wouldn't want to buy food or clothes sold by Blacks.

the
the
1.

FIRE AND FURY

Racial tensions and divides still existed, however. On 18 January 1981 thirteen Black teenagers died in a fire during a party in New Cross, London, in a tragedy that stunned the Black community. Many believed the fire was started deliberately as a racist attack and demonstrations were held to protest against a suspected police cover-up. Later that year, the police launched operation Swamp 81, a mass stop-and-search campaign which used an ancient law to arrest Blacks on 'suspicion'. They could be arrested, tried and jailed without any proof of committing a crime. Four days after Swamp 81 began, there were major street battles between Black youths and the police. The riots started in Brixton, south London, but spread to Birmingham, Liverpool and Manchester. The law was repealed in August 1981.

POWER TO THE PEOPLE

After the conflicts, Black activists began entering local politics in large numbers, ensuring that Blacks would be represented in government and their voices heard. They won control of many local councils across Britain. In the general election of 1987, four Black British people were elected to become Members of Parliament: Keith Vaz, Bernie Grant, Paul Boateng and Diane Abbott.

Newly elected MPs (left to right) Paul Boateng, Bernie Grant, Keith Vaz and Diane Abbott.

BLACK LIVES MATTER
AND GEORGE FLOYD

On 25 May 2020, George Floyd, an African American, died during a controversial arrest. He had bought a packet of cigarettes from a grocery shop in Minneapolis, Minnesota, and returned to his car. However, the shopworker thought that Floyd had paid with a fake note and called the police.

"I CAN'T BREATHE"

The police arrived and arrested Floyd, dragging him from his car. Once on the ground, one of the four officers, Derek Chauvin, placed his knee on Floyd's neck. Passers-by, shocked by the violence, took their phones out and began filming. Their cameras captured the last moments of George Floyd's life. Chauvin kept his knee on Floyd's neck for more than nine minutes. Before dying, Floyd had told the police repeatedly that he could not breathe.

TAKE TO THE STREETS

On social media, the footage captured by the passers-by was widely watched and shared. It caused an immediate uproar against racism and police brutality towards Black people, which spread around the world. New Black Lives Matter protests were planned in response to the tragedy.

The protests began on 26 May 2020 in the Minneapolis–Saint Paul area of Minnesota and quickly spread across the US and to over 2,000 cities and towns in over 60 countries. In some places, protesters laid on the road, chanting "I can't breathe". Between 15 million and 26 million people participated at some point in the demonstrations in the United States – the largest protests in US history and attended by millions of white, as well as Black, protesters.

A mural of George Floyd in Oakland, California, USA.

As the protests happened during the COVID-19 pandemic, protesters risked catching the disease by gathering. However, many felt that they had no choice but to protest, despite the risks.

TRUMP TALKS

Donald Trump, then US president, did contact Floyd's family to offer his condolences. However, he also tweeted that the protesters were 'THUGS' and warned them that the National Guard were ready to shoot them if they did not keep the protests peaceful.

The global uproar that followed the protests led to the four policemen being dismissed from work. Important reform to policing across the US was undertaken as a direct result of the protests, with many forces announcing a ban on choke holds and greater scrutiny of police actions. In April 2021, Derek Chauvin, the police officer who knelt on George Floyd's neck, was found guilty of murder.

HOPE FOR THE FUTURE?

In January 2021, Joe Biden was inaugurated as president of the United States. Many hoped that his election will put an end to the racial tension of the Trump presidency. Moreover, the elected vice president, Kamala Devi Harris, made history in two ways. She is the first woman to be elected to the vice presidency of the United States. Of Jamaican and Tamil heritage, she is also the first woman of colour to hold this position.

US Vice President Kamala Harris takes the oath of office on 20 January 2021.

BLACK LIVES MATTER
IN THE UK

Inspired by the protests across the USA, in May and June 2020, Black Lives Matter protests involving thousands of young Black and white people took place in London and in UK cities including Bristol, Cardiff, Edinburgh, Glasgow, Manchester and Nottingham.

BRITISH VICTIMS

The British protests focused on George Floyd, but also on Black British people who had faced police brutality and injustice in Britain such as Sarah Reed, who was assaulted by a policeman in 2012. She struggled with her mental health for years later. She later killed herself while in prison.

FAMOUS SUPPORTERS

Support for the Black Lives Matter movement came from high profile individuals and groups. Actor John Boyega attended and spoke at one of the protests. F1 driver Lewis Hamilton wore a black helmet emblazoned with the words 'Black Lives Matter' during the 2020 racing season, while across sport participants kneeled, or 'took the knee', before events as a symbol of solidarity with the movement. Diversity, the modern dance troupe, performed a powerful choreographed dance on *Britain's Got Talent* in support of the Black Lives Matter message.

Black Lives Matter protests in London

Lewis Hamilton and other drivers take the knee before the F1 2020 Spanish Grand Prix.

TOPPLING STATUES

The protests in Bristol focused on the statue of Edward Colston. Once regarded as a great philanthropist, Colston contributed greatly to the history of Bristol during the 17th and 18th centuries. However, historians have since learned that he was a human trafficker and slave trader. To chants of 'Take it down', protesters pulled down his statue during the protest, rolled it along a road, and eventually pushed it into Bristol Harbour.

TEACHING BLACK HISTORY

At some demonstrations, protesters carried banners that stated 'Decolonise the curriculum'. For many years, Black intellectuals have tried to encourage more teaching of Black history and heritage. A decolonised curriculum does not just include the history and heritage of white men; it includes the history and heritage of other peoples as well. As the media focused on the protests, the need to decolonise the curriculum was discussed by politicians and academics.

REPAIRING THE PAST

As the Black Lives Matter protests received publicity, major companies such as Lloyds of London and Greene King, some of whose wealth had originally come from the slave trade (see p.28–39) announced they would donate money to Black charities. The BBC removed the comedy series *Little Britain* from its playlist because of its blackface content. Other major companies increased their Black heritage staff training and reviewed their policies and practices. Finally, people in the UK bought more books by Black authors. For the first time ever, Black women writers, Reni Eddo-Lodge and Bernardine Evaristo, topped the UK best-sellers list.

Protesters throw the statue of slaver Edward Colston into Bristol harbour in June 2020.

Bernandine Evaristo, bestselling author of *Girl, Woman, Other*

BLACK HISTORY
TODAY

Compared to the position of Black people just a century ago, prospects and opportunities today are far brighter. There is still much more to do, however.

PROGRESS

By 1994 the last bastion of anti-Black prejudice, South Africa, was under Black majority rule. By 1997 Kofi Annan, a Ghanaian, was Secretary General of the United Nations. In 2008 the world celebrated the seismic election of Barack Obama as president of the United States. Black people work in all areas of employment, from engineering and finance to education and medicine. Black actors, musicians and sportspeople are globally famous. The world appears to be moving towards greater equality. But the deaths of Stephen Lawrence and Trayvon Martin and, crucially, the institutional treatment of their killers, proved there is much more to be achieved.

POVERTY

In the 21st century, the biggest single challenge facing Black people globally is poverty. Every individual Black person is not poor of course, but poverty disproportionately affects Black people and in doing so limits their opportunities from birth onwards. We have already seen that mass enslavement by Europeans opened a huge wealth gap between the descendants of the enslavers and the descendants of the enslaved. Colonisation by Europeans added to and increased this wealth gap. Nowhere in the Black world has this wealth gap been closed. Many African countries still have dirt roads, crumbling infrastructure, few schools and shabby hospitals, while poverty allows religious extremism and conflict to flourish.

Global Black musical superstars Beyoncé and Jay-Z on stage.

Water poverty remains a critical issue in many African countries.

RACISM

This poverty is at the root of other social problems. Firstly, people in the wealthier countries of Europe or North America sometimes blame Black people themselves for these poor living conditions, and not the Europeans who first impoverished them. This is a major reason why anti-Black prejudice exists. Secondly, many people in poor countries, if they get the opportunity, will come to live in Europe or North America, seeking a better life. Once there, they are seen to compete against the people already there for jobs, housing, education and healthcare. Racists claim that allowing Black people into a country makes it harder for white people already there to access these things that they see as rightfully theirs. This is another significant cause of anti-Black prejudice.

LEARN FROM THE PAST

Black history matters most when we study it, learn from it and are inspired by it. Throughout history, we have seen that Black people have always stood up for their rights, in the face of often intolerable oppression. This determination and optimism will be needed as the battle for true equality goes on.

Dr Martin Luther King's words and deeds live on. Every year, his birthday is celebrated as a public holiday in the USA.

TEACHING BLACK HISTORY

The teaching of Black history can be easily integrated into history lessons and not just restricted to lessons during Black History Month.

At **Key Stage One,** the National Curriculum advises that children should be taught

- "Changes within living memory". The content that fits this criterion is very broad. Teachers keen to include Black content could give the simple example of buying food. At one time, foods aimed at African and Caribbean people in Britain were only available from market stalls or specialised African Caribbean shops. Now, mainstream supermarkets sell these widely.

- "Events commemorated through festivals or anniversaries". This could include commemorations of importance to the Black community. For example, the Notting Hill Carnival is regarded as the biggest cultural event in the Black British calendar.

- "The lives of significant individuals in the past who have contributed to national and international achievements." The document even recommends teaching Mary Seacole, the 19th century nurse, and Rosa Parks, the African American civil rights fighter.

- "Significant historical events, people and places in their own locality." There are specialists in Black History that conduct walking tours of local areas that highlight the local Black history content. In some cases, the Black History content is marked by blue plaques erected by English Heritage and by Black community organisations such as Nubian Jak. These specialists work with schools, and hold walking tours, coach tours and Black History of London cruises up and down the Thames.

At **Key Stage Two**, the National Curriculum advises that children should be taught about:

- "The Roman Empire and its impact on Britain … including Hadrian's Wall". This is an opportunity to learn about the African emperor of Rome, Lucius Septimius Severus, who was responsible for rebuilding and fortifying the wall. Moreover, he died in York.

- "Britain's settlement by Anglo-Saxons and Scots". This could include Christian conversion. This provides an opportunity to include the African cleric who helped spread Christianity during the Anglo-Saxon era, known as the Abbot Hadrian.

- "The achievements of the earliest civilisations e.g., Ancient Egypt". In this book, we have dedicated pages to show the achievements of Ancient Egypt placed within its correct African context.

- "A non-European society that provides contrasts with British history such as Benin (West Africa) c. 900-1300 CE." This offers another opportunity to include early African history into the mainstream teaching of school history.

At **Key Stage Three**, the National Curriculum advises that pupils should be taught:

- "Social, cultural and technological change in post-war British society". This is a direct reference to the Windrush generation, wider new Commonwealth immigration and the arrival of East African Asians. This book includes some of this content. More detailed content could include a look at politician Enoch Powell and his 'Rivers of Blood' Speech, white subcultures that show Black influences including the mods, skinheads and punks, and Black British success in literature, music, drama and art.

- "Britain's transatlantic slave trade: its effects and its eventual abolition." This book includes much of this content.

- "At least one study of a significant society or issue in world history and its interconnections with other world developments … USA in the 20th Century." This includes the African American civil rights struggle. Again, this book has information on this.

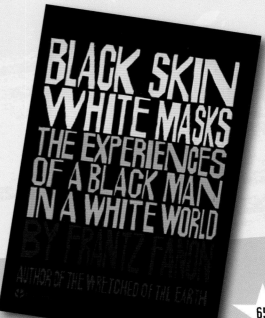

GLOSSARY

Abolition: The formal ending of the slave trade.

Activist: Someone who works to bring about social or political change.

Afrikaans: One of the official languages of South Africa and related to Dutch.

Archaeologist: Scholar who studies and interprets the material traces of the human past.

Artefact: Any object made by humans.

Black Power: A political slogan and a name for various ideologies aimed at achieving self-determination for people of African descent who live outside Africa.

Blackface: When a white performer makes up their face to look like a Black person.

Boycott: To refuse to deal with an organisation and its services.

Choke hold: To restrain a person by holding them around the neck.

Civil rights: The rights of a person to fair and equal treatment, regardless of their race, religion or gender.

Civilisation: A high point of human culture where city living, government structures and iron-using technologies exist.

Colonialism: The practice whereby more powerful countries or states take over less powerful ones to increase their own territory and profit from the colony's resources.

Colony: A country or land controlled politically by a more powerful country that has conquered it.

Conquer: Take over a place by force.

Democratic Party: One of the two major political parties in the US.

Decolonise: To grant independence to a colony.

Deport: To force someone to leave a country.

Diaspora: The dispersion or spread of any people from their original homeland. The Black diaspora refers to Black people who live outside Africa, especially those in the Americas, the Caribbean and Europe.

Discriminate: To treat a person or group of people better or worse than others.

Dynasty: A line of rulers belonging to the same ruling family.

Emancipation: The freeing of a group of people from the control of another group.

Empire: A group of nations or territories under the control of a single ruler.

Enslave: To make someone a slave.

Genocide: The deliberate killing of a group of people because of their ethnicity, nationality, religion or colour.

Indigenous: To be the first and original inhabitants of a place.

Kush: Ancient civilisation in Sudan that flourished between c.2500 BCE and CE 350.

Maroon: A name given to runaway Black slaves.

Medieval: Relating to the period of history between around the 5th and 15th centuries CE.

Middle Kingdom Egypt: Regarded as the second chapter of Ancient Egyptian history, it refers to the time of the 11th and 12th dynasties when 11 pharaohs of a united Egypt ruled.

Middle Passage: The route that slave ships took across the Atlantic from West Africa to America and the Caribbean.

New Kingdom Egypt: Regarded as the third chapter of Ancient Egyptian history, it refers to the time of the 18th, 19th and 20th dynasties when 31 pharaohs of a united Egypt ruled.

Old Kingdom Egypt: Regarded as the first chapter of Ancient Egyptian history, it refers to the time of the first six dynasties when the first 50 pharaohs of a united Egypt ruled.

Nationalism: This word has more than one meaning. The African nationalists of the 1950s to 1980s supported the political independence of their people from European colonial rule.

Native Americans: The indigenous inhabitants of North America.

Nubia: General term for the land immediately south of the Ancient Egyptian border. It includes the civilisations in this region: Ta-Seti, Kush, Makuria and Alwa.

Obelisk: A tall stone pillar, built to commemorate a person or event.

Occupy: To take up possession of a place.

Ore: Rock or earth with traces of metal in them.

Papyrus: A type of paper made from the stems of water plants.

Pandemic: A disease that affects many people over a widespread area.

Philanthropist: A wealthy person who gives their money and help to people and organisations in need.

Plantation: A large area of land where crops such as tobacco, sugar and cotton are grown.

Protest: To show publically that you disagree with something, for example by holding a rally or march.

Quatrain: A verse or poem that is four lines long.

Racism: The belief that certain races are superior to others and the behaviour or actions that result from this belief.

Reparation: The action of making amends for a wrong one has done, by paying money or other aid to those who have been wronged. Reparations for slavery is the idea that payment should be made to the descendants of Africans who were enslaved as part of the slave trade by the governments and institutions that profited from the enslaved labour.

Segregation: The practice of keeping people apart, often due to their race.

Self-government: When a country or state is governed by its own people.

Stele: An upright stone slab or pillar with writing carved into it.

Tomb: A burial place.

Trade: The practice of selling and buying goods.

Treaty: An agreement.

Underground Railroad: The network of secret routes and safe houses created in the US in the 19th century to be used by enslaved people in the southern states to escape to freedom in the northern states and Canada.

Ward: An area of a town or city that is controlled by the same administration.

White supremacy: The belief that white people are superior to all other people.

FURTHER INFORMATION

BOOKS

Black History series by Dan Lyndon (Franklin Watts, 2020)

Civil Rights Stories: Racial Equality by Anita Ganeri (Franklin Watts, 2021)

I Have a Dream: Martin Luther King and the Fight for Equal Rights by Anita Ganeri (Franklin Watts, 2016)

The History of the African and Caribbean Communities in Britain by Professor Hakim Adi (Wayland, 2020)

The Interesting Narrative and Other Writings by Olaudah Equiano (Penguin Classics, 2003)

Young, Gifted and Black: Meet 52 Black Heroes From Past and Present by Jamia Wilson and Andrea Pippins (Wide Eyed Editions, 2018)

WEBSITES

www.blackhistory4schools.com
A comprehensive collection of articles, activities and resources on the theme of Black history.

www.blackhistorymonth.org.uk
A celebration of Black history, heritage and culture in the UK.

https://africanamericanhistorymonth.gov/
A website that honours the contributions of African-Americans to the USA.

www.liverpoolmuseums.org.uk/ism/slavery/
A comprehensive history of the slave trade.

www.ancientegypt.co.uk
The British Museum's website on ancient Egypt includes a wealth of topics, from pyramids to hieroglyphics.

www.metmuseum.org/toah/hd/wsem/hd_wsem.htm
Overviews of the West African Empires from the Met Museum in New York.

www.sahistory.org.za/article/history-apartheid-south-africa
A look at the history of apartheid in South Africa.

www.bbc.co.uk/worldservice/africa/features/storyofafrica/index.shtml
An exploration of African history through the ages. Also available as an audio recording.

TIMELINE

NOTE: Most Egyptologists accept the dates shown in this timeline but some dispute them, citing archaeological evidence that indicates moving the dates back in time by about 2,000 years or more. So the Old Kingdom Period dates would be 5660–4188 BCE; Middle Kingdom Period 3448–3182 BCE and New Kingdom Period 1709–1095 BCE. The earliest dates are often very unsecure whichever dating system you follow, as dates are only certain after 664 BCE.

Pre-history

6.5 million years ago *The human story begins in Africa, where the first apes to walk upright evolve in East and South Africa.*

200,000 years ago *The first modern humans, Homo sapiens, evolve in Africa.*

100,000 years ago *Modern humans (Homo sapiens) start to move out of Africa and settle in other parts of the world.*

Dates BCE (Before Common Era – years before 1 BCE/CE 1)

7500 The first settlers arrive in the Nile Valley. At this time, higher rainfall means there is far less desert and far more green areas of plant growth. The climate changed over the next few thousand years, becoming much drier.

c.3400 Birth of kingship in the Nubian kingdom of Ta-Seti.

3300 Ancient Egyptian people use hieroglyphs (picture writing) to label goods.

3100 Menes (also known as Narmer) becomes the first pharaoh of a unified Egypt.

3100–2181 Old Kingdom Period of ancient Egyptian history.

2670 Pharaoh Djoser rules Egypt and orders that the first step pyramid at Saqqara be built.

2555–2539 The Great Pyramid at Giza is built for Pharaoh Khufu.

2500–1500 The kingdom of Kush flourishes in what is now northern Sudan.

c. 2335 The *Pyramid Texts* are written during the reign of Pharaoh Unas.

2181–2040 First Intermediate Period in ancient Egyptian history. Egypt is no longer unified and is ruled by different leaders.

2040–1786 Middle Kingdom Period of ancient Egyptian history. Pharaoh Mentuhotep II reunifies Egypt.

2000 Evidence for people smelting iron in the area of modern Nigeria.

1786–1550 Second Intermediate Period of ancient Egyptian history.

1560–1080 New Kingdom Period of ancient Egyptian history. Egyptian pharaohs build elaborate tombs in the Valley of the Kings. They rule from the city of Thebes.

1473–1458 Reign of Queen Hatshepsut, a famous female pharaoh.

1322 Death of Pharaoh Tutankhamen.

1292–1190 Pharaoh Ramesses II rules Egypt for thirty years, during which time Egypt becomes prosperous.

1080–664 Third Intermediate Period of ancient Egyptian history.

663 The Assyrians conquer Egypt.

c.550 Temple of Almaqah is built in the city of Yeha, Ethiopia.

525 The Persians conquer Egypt.

332 The Greeks, led by Alexander the Great, conquer Egypt and rule it for the next 300 years.

c.100 Axum becomes a great trading city.

30 The forces of Cleopatra VII are defeated by the army of the Roman Empire. Egypt becomes a province of the Roman Empire.

1 BCE/CE 1 Birth of Jesus Christ.

Dates CE (years after Common Era 1 BCE/CE 1)

30 Death of Jesus Christ. The religion of Christianity spreads to parts of Africa during the 1st and 2nd centuries.

c.300 Ancient Ghana becomes a kingdom.

330 Christianity becomes the state religion of Ethiopia.

350 King Ezana of Axum invades Kush.

570 Birth of Muhammad (pbuh) in Saudi Arabia.

639 Arabians invade and occupy Egypt. They conquer all of North Africa by 708.

c.700 The kingdom of ancient Ghana becomes an empire.

c.750 Mosques appear for the first time on the East African coast as Islam spreads.

c.850 The Igbo-Ukwu culture flourishes in eastern Nigeria.

c.900 Igodo establishes the First Dynasty of Benin.

c.1000 Queen Oluwo paves the city of Ile-Ife, Yoruba.

c.1085 People begin to build Great Zimbabwe, the capital of the Munhumutapa Empire.

1180 Emperor Lalibela begins the construction of the underground churches in Lalibela in Ethiopia.

1240–1433 Kingdom of Mali at its greatest.

c.1300 The Yoruba cities grow in size and wealth.

1324 Mansa Musa of Mali (and 60,000 other people) go on a pilgrimage to Mecca – the greatest pilgrimage in history.

1331 Ibn Battuta visits the East African coast.

1375–1591 The Songhai Empire is at its height.

1441 The Portuguese begin to raid Africa in order to capture people and make them into slaves. This ultimately culminates in the transatlantic slave trade that lasts for over 400 years.

1482 The Portuguese build Elmina Castle in Ghana.

1492 Christopher Columbus visits the Americas. The arrival of colonists in the Americas led to the genocide of the local people.

1505 Portuguese forces burn the Swahili cities of Kilwa and Mombassa.

1562 Englishman Sir John Hawkins becomes an important slave trader.

1576 Amina becomes ruler of Zaria. She conquers vast territories in the Nigeria region.

1591 The Moroccans invade Songhai.

1595 Enslaved Africans in Brazil establish the all-Black Palmares state.

1629 Emperor Mavhura becomes the puppet ruler of Munhumutapa on behalf of the Portuguese.

1655 Maroon communities are established in Jamaica by escaped slaves.

1787 The Society for the Abolition of the Slave Trade forms in Great Britain. Some US states abolish slavery.

1789 Olaudah Equiano writes *The Interesting Narrative of the Life of Olaudah Equiano, the African.*

1791 Enslaved Africans in Haiti revolt against the French. Eventually they gain freedom.

1807 The Slave Trade Abolition Act is passed in the British Houses of Parliament.

1831–1832 Sam Sharpe leads the Emancipation War in Jamaica against the British.

1838 Britain finally abolishes the mass enslavement of Africans.

1861–1865 American Civil War. Slavery abolished in the USA.

1879 The Zulus defeat the British invaders at Isandlwana in southern Africa.

1884–1885 European powers at the Berlin Conference agree a plan to seize control of all Africa – the Scramble for Africa.

1896 The US government enforces segregation against its Black citizens.

1897 The British army invades Benin.

1900 Henry Sylvester Williams leads the first Pan-African Conference in London.

1914–1918 First World War.

1919 Dr Du Bois leads the first of five Pan-African Congress meetings.

1920 The UNIA holds its first convention in New York, USA. 1939–1945 Second World War.

1941 The Atlantic Charter agrees that imperial colonies should be allowed to choose their own government.

1945 The Fifth Pan-African Congress in Manchester, Great Britain, calls for independence for colonial Africa.

1948 Apartheid is established across South Africa, discriminating heavily against its Black population. Caribbeans arrive at Tilbury Docks in Essex, UK, on the *Empire Windrush*.

1950s–1960s The US Black civil rights movement is very active.

1951 Elijah Muhammad recruits Malcolm X to the Nation of Islam.

1957 Dr Nkrumah becomes first president of an independent Ghana.
Most African countries gain independence within the next few years.

1959 Claudia Jones launches the first Caribbean Carnival at St Pancras Hall, Central London.

1960s The Black civil rights movement is active in the UK.

1962 Jamaica and Trinidad & Tobago become independent of Britain.
Most of the Caribbean islands gain independence within the next few years.

1963 Dr Martin Luther King leads the March on Washington D.C, USA.

1963 Paul Stephenson leads the Bristol Bus Boycott against the Colour Bar in Great Britain.

1974 Angola and Mozambique defeat Portuguese colonialism and win independence.

1981 Thirteen Black teenagers burn to death in a suspicious fire in New Cross, London, UK.

1987 Black British people become Members of Parliament for the first time.

1993 Stephen Lawrence is murdered in London, UK.

1994 Nelson Mandela becomes president of South Africa.

2008 Barack Obama becomes president of the USA.

2011 The shooting of Mark Duggan, a Black British man, at the hands of the police, leads to riots across the UK.

2012 Trayvon Martin is killed in the USA.

2013 The *#BlackLivesMatter* movement is formed.

2016 National Football League player Colin Kaepernick protests against racial inequality in the US by kneeling during the national anthem.

2018 The US midterm elections elect more than 20 Black women to the House of Congress.

2020 The murder of George Floyd at the hands of a US policeman sparks Black Lives Matter protests all around the world.
The election of Democrats Joe Biden and Kamala Harris to the US presidency and vice presidency offer new hope for racial equality in the US.

INDEX